MARCO POLO

MILAN

AND SURROUNDINGS

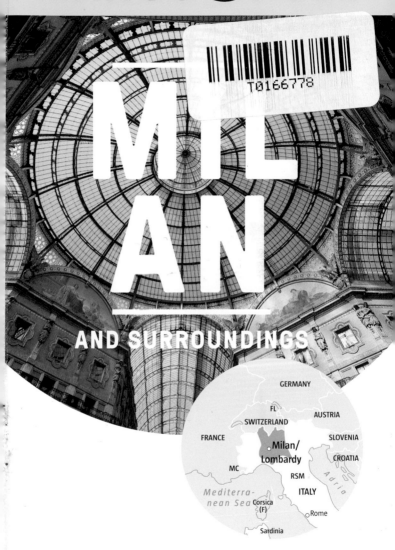

GERMANY

FL
SWITZERLAND
AUSTRIA

FRANCE
SLOVENIA

Milan/
Lombardy
CROATIA

MC
Adria

RSM
ITALY

Mediterra-
nean Sea
Corsica
(F)

Rome

Sardinia

THE
TOURING APP

shows you the way...
including routes and offline maps!

FREE!

GET MORE OUT OF YO
MARCO POLO GUIDE

IT'S AS SIMPLE AS THIS

1 go.marco-polo.com/mil

2 download and discover

GO!

WORKS OFFLINE!

SYMBOLS

INSIDER TIP	Insider Tip
★	Highlight
●●●●	Best of ...
☼	Scenic view
☺	Responsible travel: fair trade principles and the environment respected
(*)	Telephone numbers that are not toll-free

PRICE CATEGORIES HOTELS

Expensive	over 200 euros
Moderate	130–200 euros
Budget	under 130 euros

The prices are for two people sharing per night, including breakfast

PRICE CATEGORIES RESTAURANTS

Expensive	over 30 euros
Moderate	15–30 euros
Budget	under 15 euros

The prices are for a three-course dinner without drinks

DID YOU KNOW?
Sant'Ambrogio → p. 16
Spotlight on sports → p. 22
For bookworms and film buffs → p. 24
Favourite eateries → p. 54
Learn to cook alla milanese → p. 56
Local specialities → p. 58
Chinatown all'italiana → p. 64
More than a good night's sleep→ p. 80
Time to chill → p. 83
Budgeting → p. 119
Fit in the city → p. 120
Currency converter → p. 121

MAPS IN THE GUIDEBOOK
(130 A1) Page numbers and coordinates refer to the street atlas and general map at page 140/141
(0) Site/address located off the map.
Coordinates are also given for places that are not marked on the street atlas

(*A–B 2–3*) refers to the removable pull-out map

INSIDE FRONT COVER:
The best Highlights

INSIDE BACKCOVER:
Metro map

The best MARCO POLO Insider Tips

Our top 15 Insider Tips

INSIDER TIP ► A farm in the middle of the city

The idyllic *Cascina Cuccagna* at the Porta Romana is where Milan's "in crowd" likes to meet, as well as chilled singles and families, to relax and enjoy a meal. Fabulous organic kitchen and recliners on the lawn, plus a shop and a café → **p. 18**

INSIDER TIP ► Party and sleep

The whole world in one building: you'll never want to leave the *Madama Hostel*. Meals, live concerts, a popular meeting place – and at some point a bed → **p. 82**

INSIDER TIP ► All the fabulous colours of the Renaissance

The Renaissance artist Bernardino Luini was responsible for the fabulous paintings in the church *San Maurizio al Monastero Maggiore* (photo above). The Bentivoglio patron family was painted at eye level with the biblical figures – loosely based on the motto: Do good and talk about it → **p. 44**

INSIDER TIP ► A visit to the studio of a star designer

Design legend Achille Castiglioni invented his famous Mezzadro stool at the *Studio Museo Achille Castiglioni* → **p. 41**

INSIDER TIP ► World Heritage on the Adda

The premises of the historic *Crespi d'Adda* company are listed by Unesco → **p. 101**

INSIDER TIP ► Look like Steve McQueen...

... and Faye Dunaway in "The Thomas Crown Affair" – or Gregory Peck in "Roman Holiday": nothing is easier than that with the right vintage sunglasses by *Foto Veneta Ottica* → **p. 66**

INSIDER TIP ► Final resting place

Anyone who is anyone in Milan will find their final resting place on the *Cimitero Monumentale* with its 19th century "Hall of Fame" → **p. 48**

INSIDER TIP Rice as far as the eye can see

An entirely different feeling of Italy: a drive through the rice fields of the *Lomellina* (photo below); risotto lovers can make a stop at one of the farms to stock up → **p. 111**

INSIDER TIP The Italians make excellent beers!

Which you can find out for yourself with a Milan beer from the *Birrificio Lambrate*, for instance in one of the brewery's pubs → **p. 19**

INSIDER TIP Turning old into new

Making last season's fashion into an elegant new outfit: that's the concept behind ASAP – *As Sustainable As Possible* → **p. 67**

INSIDER TIP Art and enjoyment in Varese

At the *Villa Menafoglio Litta Panza di Biumo*, an art patron displays his high-carat collection with works by international contemporary artists → **p. 112**

INSIDER TIP The sewing machine maker's villa

The stylish *Necchi Campiglio* in the Art Deco design of the 1930s is to be found in a very pretty position in the city centre. Enjoy your espresso beside the original pool in the garden → **p. 34**

INSIDER TIP The bar we'd all like to have around the corner

Tiny and fabulous: at the extremely popular Corso Como, the *Blenderino* bar serves an amazing array of fabulous drinks → **p. 72**

INSIDER TIP Leonardo's vineyard

He also grew wine: the old genius is evident everywhere – even with a *Vigna di Leonardo* in the enchanting garden of the *Casa degli Antellani* → **p. 86**

INSIDER TIP The wardrobes of the Milanese ...

... house fabulous clothes that they take to the *East Market* once a month to sell → **p. 68**

BEST OF ...

GREAT PLACES FOR FREE
Discover new places and save money

● **Art for giants**

Big, bigger, biggest: new contemporary art needs more and more space. Which can be found in the former factory halls *Hangar Bicocca*, absolutely free → p. 49

● **Better living and art**

The *Casa-Museo Boschi Di Stefano* is full of paintings, ceramic sculptures as well as extremely fine Art Deco furniture. And thanks to the voluntary watchers, you are welcome to visit the museum home of the Boschi Di Stefano family of industrialists and artists completely free of charge → p. 48

● **Lovely view of the cathedral**

The cathedral roof with its fairy-tale stone forest of Gothic steeples and towers is almost close enough to touch from the *roof terrace of the La Rinascente department store*, where you can also admire the views free of charge (photo) → p. 74

● **Organ concerts**

There has been a veritable boom in organ concerts in several of Milan's churches in recent years. The concert series *Cantatibus Organis* invites everyone to free concerts (and will hopefully continue to do so, despite the challenging financial times) → p. 74

● **Park in a park**

The loveliest roses in every imaginable colour, fragrant roses, old roses, climbing roses: just behind the Villa Reale of Monza is the enchanting rose garden *Roseto Niso Fumagalli* → p. 102

● **A museum just for shoes**

During the 1970s and 1980s Vigevano was the world capital of shoes. According to that, you can admire here at the *Museo Internazionale della Calzatura* shoes worn by Renaissance princesses, Hollywood celebrities and even popes → p. 111

 Dots in guidebook refer to "Best of" tips

● *Teatro alla Scala*

The highlight of the city's social scene is the opening of the opera season which takes place in the world famous theatre (photo) on 7 December. Just how emblematic the name La Scala is for the city is shown in the way the Milanese refer to their football stadium, San Siro, as the 'La Scala of football' (photo) → p. 36

● *Basilica Sant'Ambrogio*

The city's spiritual heart beats in this wonderful Romanesque church where families wait patiently for a date to have their children baptised or to get married. When the Bishop holds a sermon here the church is filled to capacity and the Milanese recover from the stresses of worldly matters → p. 44

● *Triennale Design Museum*

Everyone knows the Sacco beanbag by the furniture brand Zanotto, the Pago Pago reversible plastic vase by Enzo Mari, or the comical, brightly-coloured shelves of Ettore Sottsass. All these iconic and playful items of Italian design can be viewed in the Design Museum → p. 41

● *Residential palaces as museums*

Many noble residential palaces – which reflect the Milanese bourgeoisie lifestyle in their architecture, their furniture and their art collections – have been turned into museums such as the *Poldi Pezzoli* → p. 36

● *Quadrilatero della Moda*

A stroll around the *Via Monte Napoleone, Via Spiga, Via Manzoni and Via Sant'Andrea*, shows that Milan is a fashion metropolis: this district is packed with exclusive boutiques! → p. 34

● *Cotoletta alla milanese*

The crumbed veal cutlet dish is the epitome of Milanese cuisine, along with its saffron risotto, and it is especially good at the osteria *Brunello* → p. 55

ONLY IN

BEST OF ...

RAIN

● *Galleria Vittorio Emanuele II*
The most beautiful and historic shopping arcade in Italy (it dates from 1867) has an ornate roof made of glass and cast iron bracing. Stroll across its magnificently patterned floor with its famous bull and then follow tradition and stand on the bull's testicles and spin around three times: this is said to bring you good luck ... (photo) → **p. 35**

● *Castello Sforzesco*
The mighty castle houses a variety of museums and interesting collections, and you can easily spend an entire rainy day here – even the walkway on the battlements is covered over → **p. 38**

● *Cooking course*
When it is pouring with rain then it is the perfect opportunity to take a short morning, afternoon or evening cooking course and learn how to make pizza, pasta, gnocchi or delicious Italian desserts → **p. 56**

● *Magnificent department stores*
In Milan's noble and elegant department stores you can while away hours admiring the displays, having extensive cosmetic consultations or enjoying a break at *Eat's*, the gourmet supermarket in the basement of the Excelsior → **p. 66**

● *Relax in a lounge bar*
When it is raining you can go to the *Living* bar, find a cosy sofa piled with cushions and settle down to take in the lush greenery of the Parco Sempione → **p. 72**

● *Museum of Natural History*
If the rain surprises you in the Giardini Pubblici, you can dash into the *Museo Civico di Storia Naturale* and spend some time with its impressive collections or in its cafeteria → **p. 96**

RELAX AND CHILL OUT
Take it easy and spoil yourself

● *Resting point (not only) for stressed parents*
Under the portico of the Rotonda della Besana with the *Museo dei Bambini* is the perfect spot for some relaxation or a picnic – helped by the pleasant bistro → **p. 97**

● *Hidden oasis of nature*
Spend a pleasant hour or so behind the picture gallery of the *Orto Botanico di Brera*. The garden measures 1.2 acre, and contains over 300 plant species → **p. 41**

● *God Save the Food*
A typical all-day eatery in the relaxed quarter of Tortona, once full of small industrial companies, now becoming increasingly popular with designer and advertising studios. Outside mealtimes, it's a good place to escape from the pressure of the busy and touristy city to enjoy an espresso and the paper → **p. 52**

● *Make-up date*
It is amazing just how relaxing it is to enjoy some professional advice when making the most of your features: Italy's most famous make-up guru *Diego dalla Palma* is based in Milan (well, where else?), and offers make-up tutorials in his cosmetic empire → **p. 68**

● *Wellness and buffet*
The Spanish defensive wall in the middle of the city is the surprising home to the *QC Terme Milano* with steaming outdoor pools, a sunbathing lawn, sauna, beauty and massages, as well as delicious refreshing buffets → **p. 83**

● *Cremona si siede*
'Cremona takes a seat' is what the locals say about themselves and while it is true that all the historic town centres in Lombardy have inviting squares with cafés – no other city takes as much pleasure in this form of relaxation as Cremona does, especially on the *Piazza del Duomo* in front of the cathedral (photo) → **p. 105**

CHILL OUT

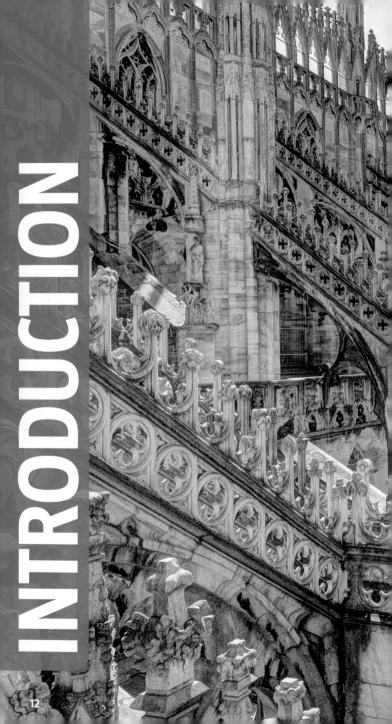

DISCOVER MILAN!

Milan has class: this cosmopolitan city has one of the best opera houses in the world, wonderfuly unique museums and a few blocks that have the highest concentration of fashion and designer shops in the world. Here you will experience the 'other' Italy, the vibrant, *energetic Italy of the 21st century*, a city of creatives and bankers. And no matter whether in a bespoke suit or in sneakers, this chic city has style in bucket loads. You need only do as the locals do to really experience Milan – have an aperitif in one of the stylish bars, go up to the roof of the cathedral, stroll through the city centre – and you will be impressed, delighted and even inspired!

There are days when the city seems to beam with pleasure – when the Torre Branca glass lift rockets you skywards from the green of the Parco Sempione and you get your first glimpse of the sunlit Castello Sforzesco from above, the *gleaming marble cathedral with its golden Madonnina* and the entire panorama of the city skyline. Towards the south, the warm, shimmering air frames the Apennine hills while in the opposite direction, behind the Arco della Pace in the north, are the peaks of the Alps, majestic against a clear blue sky. But there are also those days when the lead-grey sky is heavy, when smog streaks the windows, when the air scratches your throat and people wear their coat collars turned up. You'll just want to get away. To the nearby lakes or to Genoa by the sea, a little over an hour by car, or to the mountains, where you can stick your head above the toxic clouds.

Its prime location, between the mountains and the sea, was probably the reason why the Celts established a city ('met e leun') here in the 4th century BC. Right in the middle of the plain and at the intersection of trade routes, the location meant that it caught the attention of foreign powers who strived to have a part of this affluent city. Today Milan has approximately nine million visitors per year making it the *second-most visited city in Italy (after Rome)*. Almost two-thirds of these visitors say they are there on business. This unfortunately affects the prices in restaurants, hotels and shops, although pleasing offers can be found with online comparison and booking sites. Milan has also changed in recent years; the palette is more colourful, and pretty B&Bs and pleasant hostels are affordable alternatives. And uncomplicated snack stands. Shopping precincts and street cafés enliven the picture. Milan is becoming more and more appealing for an *interesting city trip*.

Milan is a city characterised by contrasts – there are impressive Romanesque churches juxtaposed with the purposeful financial architecture of a commercial metropolis. It is a city where everyone is always in a rush yet where creativity is still key. Along with Paris and New York, Milan is one of the global *trend-setting capitals of fashion*, which is most evident in the Quadrilatero della Moda, the fashion district behind the cathedral. It is also a city for those looking for the latest design trends – from industri-

Whether tram, bicycle or buggy: there is plenty of traffic on the Via Torino

al design to everyday objects – this is, after all, where they are all created. La Scala, Piccolo Teatro and the Pinacothecas Ambrosiana or Brera are examples of the leading role that the city plays in the fine arts sector – especially because its culture is created and maintained on large and small stages, in studios, in media and publishing companies and is not just confined to museums. Milan is also home to the phenomena of mass culture such as advertising and *football* (Inter! Milan!) and with its seven universities, and numerous technical institutes, it is also the Italian capital of technology and research. The clubs and music cafés buzz with music and people all year round, just like the clubs in Rimini at high season, only trendier, less provincial and far more expensive.

> **In Milan you experience the 'other', vibrant Italy**

Milan may also be the stronghold for the political populism of Silvio Berlusconi and his Popolo della Libertà party but by the same token, the judicial campaign against corruption and illegal party financing – the Mani pulite or 'clean hands' – got underway here in the early 1990s. There is a strong public spirit; people are committed to their city, their own particular suburb. For example, the *well-functioning waste separation system*.

Milan is not an easy city, and not just with regard to the climate (muggy summers and wet and icy winters) it is also noisy late into the night, and yet there are also enchanting nooks and *hidden quiet places right in the city centre*, such as the small park

in the Via Giardini or Donato Bramante's Cloister of the Santa Maria delle Grazie. This city is fast-paced, efficient and business-minded, but also has a big heart, it is a city that cares for its elderly and its youth, something that is evident in the large number of volunteer organisations. Milan is also unashamedly demanding and ambitious, a place where entrepreneurs, newcomers and career changers can flourish and succeed. Its church, the Basilica di Sant'Ambrogio, observes local traditions, and at the same time as a global trading platform is *more cosmopolitan than any other Italian city*. The local dialect is as much at home here as foreign languages are. In this culturally diverse city there are people from all over the world, such as the Chinese that live mostly on the Via Paolo Sarpi or the Africans on the Porta Venezia and of course English has long been the financial capital's lingua franca.

The city is still regarded as the industrial centre of Italy. This was, however, long ago, as is evidenced by the silent factories on the Via Procaccini where the cultural institutions and communications centres such as Fabbrica del Vapore are now taking up residence. The former Ansaldo locomotive works is now home to the *stage workshops of La Scala, Milan's temple to opera*. A new

All the latest design trends

university, several research facilities and even a music theatre, the Teatro degli Arcimboldi, and the exciting exhibition halls with contemporary art known as Hangar Bicocca have breathed new life into the former premises of the Pirelli tyre company in Bicocca. A large number of multi-storey administrative centres are being built in the centre, including Porta Nuova near Garibaldi railway station. And *well-known architects are building three 240-m/790-ft skyscrapers* on the former exhibition site of the Fiera, while in 2005, Europe's biggest exhibition site was opened on the western outskirts of the city at Rho to a design by Massimiliano Fuksas. Milan is in the process of radically changing its skyline.

The city seems to be *more dynamic and energetic than* ever and its leading role as Italy's financial and the economic epicentre is evidenced by the large number of companies and service enterprises that have their offices and headquarters here. Ten per cent of Italy's gross national income is generated in Milan and the unemployment rate is only half that of the national average. The city has a pop. of 1.3 million but the surrounding urban areas have merged with Milan to create a single metropolis, adding a further 5 million people. Every day 800,000 people commute into the city – turning the hunt for a parking space into an adventure.

You'll encounter names that still resonate today: the opera composer *Giuseppe Verdi* (1813–1901), whose triumphs were celebrated at La Scala. It is almost impossible to understand today that opera used to be enjoyed by the masses. Or the esteemed writer Alessandro Manzoni (1785–1873), whose Milanese novel *The Betrothed* (I Promessi Sposi) has been called the most famous and widely read novel in the Italian language. The all-round genius Leonardo da Vinci (1452–1519), sci-

SANT'AMBROGIO

Saint Ambrose was born in Trier, Germany, in 340 BC; he was first made Governor of Milan and later selected by the people to become Milan's bishop. As bishop, Ambrose had to deal with the constant tension between imperial and church interests, which he accomplished with great diplomatic skill. His reform of the liturgy (Ambrosian Rite) is still practiced today. And every year on the 7th of December his birthday is celebrated in Milan with the Feast of St Ambrose: La Scala marks the opening of its opera season and the stalls on the square in front of the church celebrate with festive cheer.

Guiseppe Verdi's tomb: the composer was a celebrity in 19th century Milan

entist, engineer, architect, artist and city icon, is omnipresent: he spent 20 years in Milan, and in that time created the most famous wall painting of all times, the "Last Supper", at the church and convent of Santa Maria delle Grazie.

Milan is opening up, becoming more colourful and more relaxed: young people are opening relaxed pubs and unusual shops, and a number of exciting museums have opened in recent years such as the Museo del Novecento, MUDEC and the Fondazione Prada *rediscovering old parts of the city*. There is one event after another, involving music, food, sports – and fashion and design, of course – and the whole city is involved, the palazzi and lofts, and yes, even the roof of the cathedral. Set

> **Enchanting courtyards and masterpieces of art**

off on a treasure hunt; almost everything is within walking distance. Through the portals of the palazzi you'll discover hidden garden oases, while grey façades open up to reveal *enchanting courtyards*. Tiny architectural gems from bygone centuries are hidden behind anonymous corners. And yet there is nothing museum-like about the city; it very much lives in the here-and-now.

Milan also shines when it gets dark: at night when lights illuminate the cathedral, its pale stone gleams brilliantly, the blue roof of La Scala's administration building shimmers secretively and the Castello Sforzesco is beautifully ablaze with white light.

1 Hidden Places

Very special places Time and again, culture *diggers* set off, unearthing forgotten places – often even finding them under the asphalt. And they breathe new life into them. For instance, the 1920s public baths in the lovely Art Deco style: head down to *Cobianchi (www.circolocobianchiduomo.it)*, now occupied by a literary association that also arranges exhibitions, and on to the cathedral square, corner Via Silvio Pellico. There is another old public baths, *Albergo Diurno Venezia (open for cultural events)*, under the Piazza Oberdan at the Porta Venezia metro station *(photo left)*. On the Piazza XXV Aprile, beside the Porta Garibaldi is an unassuming stairway down to the gallery *Grossetti Arte Contemporanea (www.grossettiart.it)* with contemporary art. It is situated on the remains of the old Spanish town wall. The medieval Basilica San Giovanni in Conca has long since been demolished, but its atmospheric *Roman crypt (Tue–Sun 9.30am–5.30pm; photo right)* is still under the asphalt of the Piazza Missori, corner Via Albricci.

Go green

Country outing in the city Feel the grass under your feet, no stress, simple. And on the table, products from estates in the surrounding area. The most tranquil idyll is in the middle of the city: the ⚫ **INSIDER TIP** *Cascina Cuccagna (www.cuccagna.org)* by the Porta Romana with shops, a café, sun loungers on the lawn, a hotel, and superior organic food *(www.unpostoamilano.it)*. Home-grown ingredients are used for the dishes served in the idyllic garden eatery ⚫ *Erba Brusca (Alziaia Naviglio Pavese 286 | www.erbabrusca.it)* on the Naviglio Pavese canal. For refreshments in the north, people head for the Cascina Martesana *(Via Luigi Bertelli 44 | www.cascinamartesana.com)* as they cycle along the Martesana canal *(photo)* or meet up for a barbecue.

There are lots of new things to discover in Milan. A few of the most interesting are listed below

Not-so-small beer

Birra artigianale Freshly brewed unpasteurised beer – *chiara, bionda, rossa, scura* – from small *birrifici*, breweries, has become something of a cult. For Alex Marelli of the *Hopsbeershop (Via Montebello 14)*, the small, very well-stocked beer shop and pub in Brera, the craft beers from Bergamo are the best. The beer boom started in Milan at the INSIDER TIP *Lambrate brewery (www.birrificiolambrate.com)* in the suburb of Lambrate with two popular pubs in Lambrate at Via Adelchi 5 and Via Golgi 60. The brewery BQ Birra Artigianale of Sondrio operates a number of pubs, one of them on the *Naviglio Grande (Alzaia Naviglio Grande 44 | www.bqmilano.it)*. The first Italian monastery beer also hailed from Milan, where Benedictine monks brewed it on the *Cascina Cascinazza (birracascinazza.it)* estate.

Young fashion talents

Making designer dreams come true Up-and-coming fashion creators are supported by the *Camera Nazionale della Moda Italiana (www.cameramoda.it)*, e. g. with projects such as the Fashion Hub Market, where they are able to present their collections at the *Milano Moda Donna*. During the Fashion Weeks, new labels are shown at the *White Milano (www.whiteshow.it)* at the Superstudio Più in the Zona Tortona. Young designers blaze their own trails with ♲ recycled and naturally processed materials with slogans such as *Slow Fashion* or *So critical so fashion* at events such as the annual *Fa la cosa giusta (www.falacosagiusta.org)* in March.

IN A NUTSHELL

HAPPY HOUR

The aperitif is as much a part of this city as the olive is of a Dry Martini. Whether in the „local" next door, the popular roof terrace or the chic bar of a luxury hotel, the wonderful urban ritual of the aperitivo kicks off at around 6.30pm. Also known as Happy Hour, it's when people can finally forget the stress of a hectic day, and you will experience the Milanese with friends and, yes indeed, with colleagues. They discuss the weekend trip, the next exhibition, and which new places to try out. The barkeepers work flat out, mixing Spritzes, Negronis and Moscow Mules. It's not surprising that red Campari, the base for so many drinks, was invented in Milan. Then there are elegant finger food buffets, and dishes with pasta, risotti, couscous and crudites – almost a full evening meal. Even better: olives and savouries. Because above all, the aperitivo is that magical moment when you finally put the day behind you, and look forward to a relaxed and unencumbered evening or *cena*.

THE STUFF THAT DESIGNERS' DREAMS ARE MADE OF

Take some fabric or leather, sew it into a large tear-shaped bag, and fill it with polystyrene beads. That's exactly what three young Milanese designers did – and created a seat that became a huge hit. They called it simply *sacco*, sack, although it is more commonly known as a

Photo: Designer furniture

Fashion and design, rap and aperitif: Milan is a flow heater for all kinds of style questions

bean bag. This 1960s seat has long been on display in the world's design museums, and – still in fashion – is still being produced. Off-the-wall associations, addressing ideas with no compulsion to conform, a relaxed aestheticism in daily life – all that is behind design that is „Made in Italy." And naturally, Milan is its centre. Because this isn't just where the creative minds are, but – and this is really important – where the doers are as well. These are the bold companies who are prepared to carry out the designers' wacky ideas and put them on the market. Over time, a network of adventurous manufacturers has developed around Milan in Lombardy – their names are Zanotta, Molteni, Artemide, Kartell, Cassina. Insiders speak of the „Milan model", and that it is unique in the world. You can experience this vast Lombardy design tradition at the Triennale Design Museum and in the showrooms of Artemide or Kartell. And while those in the trade meet in April for the design fair, the *Salone ernazionale del Mobile*, young talents present their projects in backyards and garages, and the whole town becomes one big, exciting studio, the *Fuorisalone*.

PRADA AND MORE

Is there anything apart from fashion? It's not enough, even for the major luxury labels. The brands that have shaped Milan's reputation as an international fashion city want more – for their city, and for their image here. They are fashion designers such as Miuccia Prada, who built up her multi-billion empire from her grandfather's leather workshop. Or Giorgio Armani, whose „deconstructed" jackets removed everything stiff and formal from the blazer, making it supple and giving it a nonchalant elegance, which has since been worn by men and women alike. These designers help to shape the Milan of today, each in their own individual way. Giorgio Armani has opened a fashion museum – the *Armani Silos* (see p. 46) and an elegant *suite hotel (Via Manzoni 31)*. Dolce & Gabbana have put their coolly pompous stamp on the *Bar Martini (Corso Venezia 15)*. Trussardi is causing a stir with a *top restaurant* and *Temporary Art Events*. Prada has gone for the most exciting spot: a spectacular exhibition centre on the southern edge of the city centre *Fondazione Prada (Largo Isarco 2)*. It is spectacular, because the star architect has cleverly combined old industrial buildings with new constructions, and exciting new art is displayed in them.

COCAINE PARTY AND THE MIDDLE FINGER

Everyone knows that coke is taken all over Milan. Over twice as much as anywhere else in Italy. How do we know? From residue analyses of the city's waste water. It's an unpleasant truth, and it was the inspiration for Italy's best-known street artist Blu who, like Britain's Banksy,

SPOTLIGHT ON SPORTS

When Milan's two football clubs gather for the Derby, more precisely for the *Derby della Madonnina* (you know, the golden statue of the Virgin Mary atop the cathedral), then the fabulous old *Stadio San Siro* (see p. 48) really starts to rock. At last – sold out, and an amazing atmosphere. The true football fan's pulse starts to race at the thought of Milan's two glorious football clubs; they continue to be assured of respect despite having shown some undeniable signs of tiredness in recent years. The city has long since been split in two at the *calcio*: the *milanisti* in *red and black stripes* are the fans of AC Milan, and in the blue-and-black stripes are the *interisti*, the followers of Inter. You're a fan from birth. Traditionally, Inter is more a matter of the left side of the heart, Milan of the right. But then, the times are a-changing. Today, the clubs both belong to Chinese investors, who have entirely different expectations. Efficiency at the game, to ensure they are restored to their former positions in the international ranking. You will find the schedules and can book tickets at *www.italysoccertickets.com*, which you can also buy them at the stadium ticket offices on the day of a match, because games are rarely, if ever, sold out.

is only known by his professional name, when he created his mural on the outside wall of the *PAC, the Pavilion of Contemporary Art*: it depicts a monstrous coke party. Opinions are very much divided, and some – including the PAC – want to paint over this particular party. But art likes to rub a little salt into the wound. The artist Maurizio Cattelan does just that with a giant middle finger in white marble that is on display outside the *Milan Stock Exchange* on the Piazza degli Affari. Needless to say, the financiers who have to look at this finger from their offices every day aren't quite so amused. The battle rages on, and somehow the otherwise rather more proper Milan displays its bolder side.

MILAN, I'LL SING TO YOU

Don't think of soppy ballads about the city, with eternal sunshine and the blue, blue sea, which it doesn't have anyway, which is why the Neapolitans do that so much better. Milan's songwriters generally have a more love-hate relationship with their city. At the moment, it's rappers like J-Ax, Fedez or Emis Killa. The latter expresses it quite clearly: *Milano male* – bad Milan, full of hypocrisy and hardness behind the pretty surface, yet still a part of him. Fedez calls his rap *Milano bene*: these are the middle-aged men with their thick briefcases in the private rooms that the doormen refuse to let him, barefoot and wearing the wrong shirt, enter. So he waits for his girl outside. A bit of gossip: Fedez has found his Milanese girl, and currently she is star blogger Chiara Ferragni.

COLOURFUL BIRDS AT THE FASHION WEEKS

He lives, the big exotic parrot that sits on the shoulder of a lady who is taking her brightly-coloured outfit for a walk along the Via Montenapoleone: so which is the more colourful bird? There is plenty going on at Fashion Weeks time in Milan: the new Moda Donna

Plan well in advance: your outfit for Fashion Week

connections are presented at the end of February and September, while it's the men's turn in January and June. And although the best-known fashion labels' shows and parties take place behind closed doors, anyone can join the party on the streets: it's simply amazing to see the colours, cuts and passion for design on display. Fur-lined leather slippers are a huge hit. The whole experience is not unlike carnival, a feeling of playfulness, and assuming a different persona for a while. The street style parade gathers outside the locations where the big names present their latest collections. Photographers, bloggers, onlookers (and that includes us) wait at the doors, cameras and smartphones at the ready, for the fashion people and models to appear when the show is over. Really, who would want to be on the guest list when you can see so many inspiring outfits just walking along the streets at this time? Calendar and locations: *www.cameramoda.it*

TOUCHING THE CLOUDS

Even the Virgin Mary is unable to stop the rise and rise of Milan. For a long time it was the rule that no building was allowed to be higher than this golden statue (it has topped the highest peak of the cathedral – 108 m/354 ft – since 1773), which is 4 m/13.1 ft high and weighs several tonnes, and is lovingly called „Madonnina" by the Milanese. The once rather low town is now rushing to emulate the metropolises of the world, and the skyline is growing and growing as if a new era had dawned. You can see it most clearly at the station, *Porta Garibaldi*. The bar was raised even further in 2010 with the high-rise buildings for the regional administration of Lombardy (161 m/528 ft), and even more so just a year later with the tower for the Unicredit bank. The 755 ft/230 m tip of Italy's tallest building today literally touches the clouds. The high-rise enclave also includes the two „green" residential towers, the ⊕ *Bosco Verticale*, the award-winning, stylish city brand for Milan green & smart. However, the favourite skyscraper of the architecture lovers is somewhere entirely different, right outside the main station: the elegant, slender tower was built in 1959 as the base of the Pirelli tyre company, and to many is the actual symbol of the modern Milan.

BLONDE SALAD

Long, silky blond hair and a passion for self-presentation, garnished with fashionable bits & pieces, plus an efficient partner you've known since school. Sounds harmless enough to be going on with, and quite satisfactory. When Chiara Ferragni launched her fashion blog *The Blonde Salad (www.theblondesalad.com)* in 2009, she never imagined that she would one day be one of the most suc-

FOR BOOKWORMS AND FILM BUFFS

In the Name of Ishmael – a thrilling and complex crime novel, by Giuseppe Genna, set in the current day Milan as well as the Milan of the 1960s.

Cabal – this is another entertaining Aurelio Zen mystery by popular crime writer Michael Dibdin (1992), this time an apparent suicide in the Vatican leads Zen to Milan and the murky world of secret societies. There is quite a bit of Italian history and also some insights into the Italian fashion world.

I Am Love – in Luca Guadagnino's 2009 film, Tilda Swinton plays the matriarch of an *haute bourgeois* Milanese family through changing times and fortunes, in the fabulous ambience of the *Villa Necchi Campiglio* (see p. 34)

Miracle in Milan – director Vittorio de Sica filmed this classic in Milan in 1951. The story revolves around Italy's national hero, Totò, who fights against greedy industrialists with the help of guardian angels and a magic dove. Because the film was a fairy tale, it was very successful.

cessful bloggers in the world. Her understanding of creative styling has won her over 6 million followers on Instagram – plus a breathtaking turnover of 8 million euros, and the figure is still rising. She earns that amount as an influencer for certain fashion labels. Fashion brands realised long ago that successful bloggers are potent advertising mediums. Chiara has gone a step further: now a brand in her own right, she has her own shoe collection and is planning her first store in Milan. She will announce when and where on her blog, in plenty of time. Incidentally, that's also where she shares all her favourite eating places in Milan and which spa she likes to visit for some pampering.

GREENER THAN YOU WOULD THINK

You can arrange to stay at the *Bosco Verticale*, Italy's best-known high-rise pair (111 m/364 ft and 78 m/255.9 ft), through Airbnb. Thousands of trees and shrubs grow vertically up its façades, which is not only delightful to look at but smart as well: it's a new eco experiment at providing natural air conditioning and producing oxygen to clean the air. And isn't it just typical of Milan, to address the battle (long overdue) against smog with such style? But the city is also doing lots of other things: there are 5000 public bikes that can be borrowed in all sorts of places to ride on an impressive 185 km/115 mi of cycle paths. And in the Italian comparison, Milan is first in car-sharing, using its (excellent) public transport system, operating methane-powered buses and cars, and one of its metro lines is even powered by solar energy. Drivers in the centre have to pay a green charge. Registrations of private cars have been declining for years, and in the European comparison, the city is

The 1959 Pirelli Tower was Milan's first *grattacielo* (skyscraper)

even better at organising its waste than Vienna. Some of the most obvious trends are organic supermarkets (e.g. NaturaSì) and restaurants, farmers' markets with organic produce, exchange platforms, and more and more young designers making a name for themselves by upcycling and recycling.

SIGHTSEEING

CITY **WHERE TO START?**

The best starting point is the central **Piazza del Duomo (131 D4)** *(💮 K5)*, as all the main sights are just a short walk away. To get there from the main train station, take the yellow Metro line 3 to San Donato and get off at the cathedral square (stop: Duomo). Car parks in the centre include the parking garage of the department store *La Rinascente (Via Agnello 13)* and *Autosilo Diaz (Piazza Armando Diaz 6)* 100m south of the cathedral square. In the city centre, the *ecopass* is mandatory (see 'Travel Tips').

You can easily fill a week with high culture, with the works of the great masters such as Leonardo da Vinci and Caravaggio. You'll find modern art in the former industrial buildings, but also in marvellous palazzi. Head to the courtyards or showrooms for the design scene. And then, of course, there's the main attraction: shopping. Hardly any other town or city is better equipped for this, with everything from luxury department stores to vintage markets

Everything is surprisingly easy to reach, and you can stroll from one attraction to the next: through the cathedral square and the grandiose Galleria Vittorio Emanuele II to the Piazza della Scala with Italy's most famous opera house. Then on to the pretty, former artists' quarter

Milan is not a city that is revealed at first glance – it is a city that wants to be explored and discovered

Brera with original boutiques, design and antiques shops. Look beyond the old roofs, and you'll see the modern high-rise buildings near Porta Garibaldi station, with parks, stores and cafés waiting for you at their feet. From the cathedral square, head north-east and in ten minutes you'll be at Quadrilatero della Moda, and the glamorous luxury stores on the Via Monte Napoleone and Piazza San Babila. It's just as short a walk to the Via Dante shopping street, and then you'll find yourself facing the impressive façade of the castle, with Milan's green lung, the Parco Sempione, beyond. Heading south-west, stroll along the Via Torino and Corso Porta Ticinese, fringed by shops, cafés, and yes, by 16 impressive ancient Roman pillars: Milan was already big and important in Antiquity, second only in position to Rome. And now you'll be in the idyllic canal quarter of Navigli. Right next door is an iron railway bridge to a former industrial and working-class district, the Zona Tortona, now the trendy area for creative minds.

DISTRICT MAP

GARIBALDI, SEMPIONE & BRERA
Page → 37

MAGENTA & SANT'AMBROGIO
Page → 42

QUADRILATERO
Page → 34

CENTRO STORICO
Page → 30

NAVIGLI
Page → 45

The map shows the location of the most interesting districts. There is a detailed map of each district on which each of the sights described is numbered.

Time, wars and – above all – the fact that the Milanese never stand still have left and leave gaps, with the most diverse building styles standing cheek by jowl: fabulous façades of the aristocratic residences of the 17th and 18th centuries alternate with the splendid residences of the turn of the century, with bizarrely decorated Liberty Palazzi from the first years of the 20th century. Then the stunners of the 1930s such as the main station, the stock exchange and the law courts. Finally, the post-war building boom, and the juxtapositioning of anonymous buildings with the ultra-elegant. And today, the glass skyline: Milan has arrived in the new millennium. And dotted throughout, here and there, ancient churches and quiet, se-

cluded spots make their own subtle statements. Indeed, the city has many faces, and it's exciting to explore them. It doesn't have the look of a typical Italian old town. A glance at a map of the city, and you'll be able to see a little of its past: history has settled in rings around the centre, which is clearly evident in today's streets and roads. There's the former circular wall, which was built under the powerful families of the Middles Ages and the Renaissance, the Visconti and the Sforza. This so-called *cerchio dei navigli*, which touches the Sant'Ambrogio, San Lorenzo and Ca' Granda, was surrounded by *navigli*, canals, until the 1930s. Under Spanish foreign rule from the middle of the 16th century until 1700, the city continued to grow, which brought the next ring: the fortification ring *cinta dei bastioni*: you can still see a piece of this city wall at one of the city gates, the Porta Romana. Tram line no. 9 follows it from the main station and passes most of the city gates, such as Porta Venezia, Porta Vittoria, Porta Ticinese to Porta Genova. Go on a treasure hunt: when a portal opens, don't be afraid to go through it – you might discover a colonnaded courtyard, a quiet garden idyll, a studio or a traditional *casa ringhiera*, Milan's unique blocks of flats with common passageways to individual homes. Lovely museums contain the treasures that have been collected in the city over the centuries: the Pinacoteca in Brera, one of the most valuable collections of paintings in Italy. Or go to the second floor of Via Giorgio Jan 15, the apartment that belongs to the industrial family *Boschi Di Stefano*, which contains so many works

of modern Italian art that you can't see any of the walls beneath them. The private museum is one of the so-called *Case Museo*, a very special Milanese treat: former private homes that are now open to the public, such as richly furnished palazzi from previous centuries, artists' studios or, right at the centre, a stylish villa from the 1930s with an enchanted garden. If you find all this beauty just too much to cope with, why not climb up onto the roofs: surrounded by statues of saints and demons, stroll over the roof terraces of the cathedral, the city and the distant Alps in your sight, and watch the hustle and bustle on the cathedral square below. The cathedral is almost close enough to touch from the roof café of the La Rinascente department store right next door. And the best place to see just how impressive the citadel is, is from the lookout tower of the Torre Branca in the Parco Sempione.

MARCO POLO HIGHLIGHTS

CENTRO STORICO

Magnet or star: in its grandezza, the cathedral is both. Its charisma has accompanied people for centuries, and it gives the city a special aura. And like a grail, its fabulous interior houses a reverent mysticism – yes, in this material city.

The treasure hunt begins on the cathedral square. The underground lines crisscross below it, and it's also where you register if you want to use one of the orange bikes. Or are looking for a ticket for a night of opera at La Scala. And you can get all the latest information from the Urban Center tourism office at the end of the Galleria Vittorio Emanuele II.

1 CA' GRANDA (131 E5) (*Ⓜ K–L 5–6*)

Students walk freely around this fabulous complex of buildings – the main home of the university since 1958 – and sit under the columns in the vast courtyards with their laptops. It's hard to imagine that for centuries, and until as recently as 1939, the poor and the diseased fought for their lives here: the "big house" was built by Francesco Sforza, the Duke of Milan, in the 15th century as the town's hospital. *Via Festa del Perdono 5 | Metro 1, 3 Duomo, Missori | tram 16, 24 | bus 77, 94*

2 SANTA MARIA NASCENTE CATHEDRAL ★ (131 D–E4) (*Ⓜ K5*)

It's not easy to get into the cathedral. There are long queues at the entrances – after all, there are 4 million visitors to it every year. But as you wait, you can use the time to admire this vast and yet surprisingly delicate construction in every imaginable shade of grey and white marble. Despite the long history of its construction, which lasted from the 14th until the 19th centuries, the generations of master builders remained loyal to the style of the Lombardy Gothic: a harmonious overall effect. Measuring 158 m/

Milan's heart beats all in white: Santa Maria Nascente

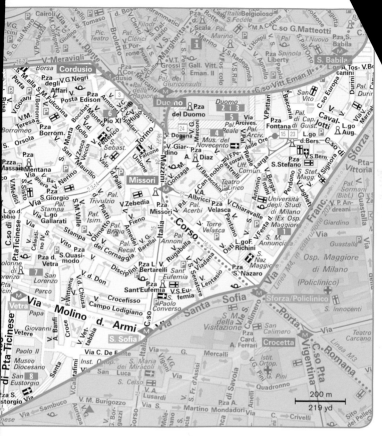

SIGHTSEEING IN THE CENTRO STORICO

1 Ca' Granda

2 Santa Maria Nascente Cathedral

3 Cathedral roof

4 Museo del Novecento

5 Palazzo Reale and
cathedral museum

6 Pinacoteca Ambrosiana

7 San Lorenzo Maggiore

8 Sant'Eustorgio

Pedestrian precinct

518 ft along the outside and with an area of 2.8 acres, the cathedral is one of the biggest churches in Christianity. The evening light falls in broken colours through the huge windows of the five-naved interior. Visitors walk through a forest of 52 pillars in this mystical light. They all stop in horror at the statue of St. Bartholo-mew (1562), whose flayed skin is wrapped around him like a cloth. Access to the ancient excavations and the foundations of the previous buildings *(daily 9am–7pm | 7 euros incl. cathedral and cathedral museum)* is in the interior near the main entrance. *Daily 8am–7pm | 3 euros incl. cathedral museum, tickets*

es beside and behind the cathedral | Piazza del Duomo | www.duomomilano.it | Metro 1, 3 Duomo

▣ 3 CATHEDRAL ROOF ☀
(131 D–E4) (*ω K5*)

Where can you climb onto the roof of a cathedral? Here, there's even a lift to take you up onto it! The views are fabulous, and you'll be up close to its stony residents, the hundreds of saints, demons and animals. As well as the 4-m/ 13.1-ft high Madonna, lovingly called the Madonnina by the Milanese. During WWII she was covered in black cloth so that bomber pilots would not be able to see her glowing golden lights. *Daily 9am–7pm, longer in summer | 9 euros (with the lift 13 euros) | Piazza Duomo, stair access at the north side in front of the department store La Rinascente, lift opposite on the south side | www.duomomilano.it | Metro 1, 3 Duomo*

▣ 4 MUSEO DEL NOVECENTO ★ ☀
(131 D–E4) (*ω K5*)

The terrace of the Palazzo dell'Arengario is where the Fascist dictator Benito Mussolini once stood to give his inflammatory speeches to the masses on the cathedral square. Today, the neon loops by Lucio Fontana, one of the greats in Modernity, shine through the windows of this elegant 1930s building, guiding you to the excellent collection of 20th century Italian art housed within. Of course, Italy also has modern masters. It starts with the futurists – the avant garde at the beginning of the century, who provided the figure on the Italian 20-cent coin. Important names are Giorgio De Chirico and Marino Marini; then followed the "poor art", the Arte Povera of the 70s, and the current video art. *Mon 2.30pm–7.30pm, Tue, Wed, Fri, Sun 9.30am–7.30pm, Thu and Sat 9.30am–10.30pm | 10 euros incl. exhibition | Via Guglielmo Macconi 1 | www.museodel novecento.org | Metro 1, 3 Duomo*

▣ 5 PALAZZO REALE AND CATHEDRAL
MUSEUM (131 D–E4) (*ω K5*)

And yes, Milan also has a palace for kings, right next to the cathedral. Napoleon once slept here, when he had himself crowned king of Italy in 1805 in the cathedral next door. Built to plans by Giuseppe Piermarini, the star builder of the 18th century, the neoclassical *Palazzo Reale* is today a site for exclusive exhibitions. At the *Museo del Duomo (Tue–Sun 10am–6pm | www.duomo milano.it)* it is fascinating to see how beautifully the cathedral's treasures, artistic statues, windows, liturgical artefacts, are displayed in the wing on the left. *Mon 2.30pm–7.30pm, Tue, Wed, Fri, Sun 9.30am–7.30pm, Thu, Sat 9.30am–10.30pm | 14 euros palace and exhibition | Piazza del Duomo 12 | www.palazzorealemilano.it | Metro 1, 3 Duomo*

▣ 6 PINACOTECA AMBROSIANA
(130 C4) (*ω J5*)

To the west of the cathedral square, business people bustle about amongst the banks and offices. But there is also a quiet little piazza leading to this historic library. When Cardinal Federico Borromeo started his art collection in 1618, he had a single mission: to make lovely works of art and the sciences accessible to all the public, not just the elite. At the Pinacoteca, one particular little picture is one of its greatest treasures: shimmering dew drops on ripe grapes next to worm holes in an apple. Life in all its beauty and transience in a basket of fruit, the *canestra di frutta*, painted by the great artist Caravaggio in 1599. And the *Biblioteca Ambrosiana* is home to the "Codex Atlanticus", 1119 sheets on which all-round genius Leonardo da Vinci recorded his studies of anatomy, physics and mechanics. They are presented digitally. *Tue–Sun 10am–6pm | 15 euros | Piazza Pio XI 2 | www.ambrosiana.eu | Metro 1, 3 Cordusio, Duomo*

7 SAN LORENZO MAGGIORE
(130 B6) *(ⓜ J6)*

South-west of the cathedral square is the lively Via Torino, and from there it's on to the Corso di Porta Ticinese. Suddenly it seems all you can see is ancient history: 16 vast columns along the pavement that date back to Antiquity, when Milan was one of the biggest cities in the Roman Empire. Behind them is the no less impressive basilica of *San Lorenzo Maggiore*. The fact that they could even be constructed is thanks to the bronze man outside on the church square, the Roman Emperor Constantine. In 1313, he decreed the freedom of all religions, and the new Christians were able to build their churches. This basilica was one of the first. The mosaic remains in a side chapel date back to the 4th century. Many centuries have passed since then, and they have been rebuilt countless times, and today are seen in the classical style of the 19th century with a dome from the Renaissance. Walk around the church, and with the park behind you, you will be able to see quite clearly, in your mind's eye, how the chapels were added. A few steps further along the Corso di Porta Ticinese, and you'll come to one of the two gates that remain from the medieval city fortification, the Porta Ticinese. *Corso di Porta Ticinese 35 | www.sanlorenzomaggiore.com | tram 3*

8 SANT'EUSTORGIO (137 E4) *(ⓜ J7)*

After the medieval city gate Porta Ticinese, you'll come to this ancient basilica. It contains four bones, and they are what

Home of the modern masters: Museo del Novecento

make it so very special to the Milanese – they are said to have belonged to the Three Wise Men. Their sarcophagus in the transept on the right is the destination of a festive procession from the cathedral that takes place every year on Epiphany, on 6 January.

Sant'Eustorgio was also founded an extremely long time ago, although today it is seen in the style of the 13th century – some of it genuine, like the church spire, some restored. If you are interested in the Renaissance, be sure to see the valuable *Portinari Chapel*. The religious works by modern artists on display at the *Museo Diocesano (chapel and museum Tue–Sun 10am–6pm | 6 euros)* in the area of the monastery is particularly impressive. *Piazza Sant'Eustorgio 1 | tram 3, 9 | bus 94*

QUADRI-LATERO

This will make any fashion victim's pulse beat faster: the density of exclusive boutiques in the ● Quadrilatero d'Oro, the "Golden Square" north-east of the cathedral square.

Armani, Dior, Gucci and all the other international luxury and fashion labels – they all have not just one, but several stores here. Limousines with dark windows and Ferraris emit their expensive growls as they make their way along the streets. The sales assistants speak Russian, Japanese, Chinese, Spanish.

It starts at the Galleria Vittorio Emanuele II and ends on the Via Monte Napoleone and its side streets. However, you will also come across elegant palaces; the nobility and upper classes once lived here – and those that can afford it still do. Some of the palazzi are now museums

with intact interiors that illustrate the sheer sophistication, the exclusivity, of how people used to live here.

■1■ CORSO VENEZIA & VIA MOZART
(131 F2–3) (*ⓜ L4*)

On the *Corso Venezia*, the former top address which stretches from the Piazza San Babila to the Porta Venezia, you'll see old palaces of the nobility such as the *Casa Fontana-Silvestri* (no. 10), which dates back to the Renaissance, the neoclassical *Palazzo Serbelloni* (no. 16) and the Art Nouveau *Palazzo Castiglioni* (no. 47). Continue beyond the Palazzo Serbelloni onto *Via Mozart*, a stylish residential area of luxurious apartment blocks from the early 20th century. Even the stairwells are worth a visit. A charming garden contains the INSIDER TIP *Villa Necchi Campiglio (Wed–Sun 10am–6pm | 10 euros | Via Mozart 14 | www.casemuseomilano.it)*, a fascinatingly styled example of how people lived in the 1930s. *Metro 1 San Babila, Palestro, Porta Venezia*

Three centuries of consumption: Galleria Vittorio Emanuele II is chic again today

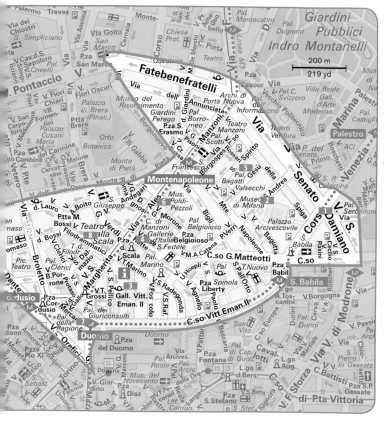

SIGHTSEEING IN THE QUADRILATERO

1 Corso Venezia & Via Mozart

2 Costume Moda Immagine
Palazzo Morando

3 Galleria Vittorio Emanuele II

4 Gallerie d'Italia

5 Museo Bagatti Valsecchi

////// Pedestrian precinct

6 Museo Poldi-Pezzoli

7 Piazza Mercanti

8 Teatro alla Scala

2 COSTUME MODA IMMAGINE PALAZZO MORANDO
(131 E2) (*ØØ L4*)

The fabulous ambience of this elegant 18th century palace contains outfits and glamorous exhibitions that provide an insight into historical and contemporary aspects of this city of fashion. *Tue–Sun 9am–1pm and 2pm–5.30pm | price of ad-* *mission depends on the exhibition | Via Sant'Andrea 6 | www.costumemodaim magine.mi.it | Metro 1, 3 San Babila, Monte Napoleone*

3 GALLERIA VITTORIO EMANUELE II
★ ● (131 D3) (*ØØ K5*)

Il salotto, the city's "drawing room", with bars, restaurants and shops, is a cosmopolitan temple made of stone, steel and glass, the first shopping mall of the 19th century. The interior measurements of the dome (highest point 47 m/154.2 ft) match those of the dome of St. Peter's Basilica in Rome. It's smart again today, now that McDonald's has moved out and Gucci has moved in. Which says it all. New additions are the *Café Marchesi* and the Il *Mercato del Duomo* food hall. You can see the roof of the Galleria from the photo gallery 🔆 *Osservatorio Prada (entrance between the Prada boutique and the Feltrinelli bookshop)*. A Campari at the bar *Camparino in Galleria* (see p. 52) at the junction between Galleria and cathedral square is a must. *Piazza del Duomo 21–23/Piazza della Scala | Metro 1, 3 Duomo*

▣ GALLERIE D'ITALIA
(131 D3) (*ØŊ K4*)

The capital purchases art: Intesa Sanpaolo, Italy's biggest baking group, focuses its collection on the art styles of the 19th and 20th centuries: The wide and diverse arch spans the period to this day in two delightful palazzi *(18th and 19th centuries)* on the Piazza della Scala. *Tue/Wed and Fri–Sun 9.30am–7.30pm, Thu 9.30am–10.30pm | 10 euros | Piazza della Scala 6 | www.gallerieditalia.com | Metro 1, 3 Duomo, Monte Napoleone*

▣ MUSEO BAGATTI VALSECCHI
(131 E2) (*ØŊ K–L4*)

The two Bagatti Valsecchi brothers wanted to live a Renaissance lifestyle – 400 years later, in the 19th century. To that end, they had their palazzo completely converted and collected valuable furniture, decorative items, art and weapons. This luxurious "cabinet of curiosities" is one of the *Case Museo di Milano (www.casemuseomilano.it)*, examples of the highly-cultivated lifestyles of the

nobility and upper classes that have been turned into museums. *Tue–Sun 1pm–5.45pm | 9 euros | Via Gesù 5/Via Santo Spirito 10 | www.museobagattivalsecchi. org | Metro 1, 3 San Babila, Monte Napoleone | tram 1 | bus 54, 94*

▣ MUSEO POLDI-PEZZOLI ★ ●
(131 D–E2) (*ØŊ K4*)

The atmosphere in this private museum in a 19th century house that is also one of the *Case Museo* makes it probably one of the loveliest museums in Milan. The rich collection of the last owner, Gian Giacomo Poldi Pezzoli, which was bequeathed to the nation following his death in 1879, includes Antonio del Pollaiuolo's famous "Portrait of a Woman" (c. 1470), now the symbol of the museum. Also worth a visit: the valuable collection in the Clock Room. *Wed–Mon 10am–6pm | 10 euros | Via Alessandro Manzoni 12 | www.museo poldipezzoli.it | Metro 3 Monte Napoleone*

▣ PIAZZA MERCANTI
(130 C3–4) (*ØŊ K5*)

Almost an Italian old town: a medieval piazza opens up just a few steps from the cathedral square. In its midst is a pillared loggia with the *Palazzo della Ragione*, the town hall of 1233, where the citizens' council used to meet. Today it is a venue for photographic exhibitions. Merchants and notaries for the purchase contracts used to meet in other buildings. To the south-west, you'll find quiet little streets such as the *Via Victor Hugo* or *Via Spadari*, antique shops and places to eat. *Metro 1 Cordusio*

▣ TEATRO ALLA SCALA ●
(131 D2–3) (*ØŊ K4*)

Probably Milan's best-known ambassador to the world: La Scala. Architect Giuseppe Piermarini had the opera house built in 1778. Initially, there was only

Damask from the 19th century, high tech from the 21st century: Teatro alla Scala opera house

standing room in the stalls; only the five horseshoe-shaped rows in the stalls had seating. Rossini, Verdi and Puccini's operas were performed in the 19th century. Singers like Enrico Caruso and Maria Callas continued the success story during the 20th century.

La Scala has become a symbol of the city. When it was destroyed by bombs during World War II, it was rebuilt immediately after the end of war – even before houses, hospitals and other public buildings were repaired. The renowned architect Mario Botta of Ticino worked on the refurbishment of La Scala from 2002 to 2004. The acoustics were greatly improved, and Botta added an elliptical construction to the 19th century administrative wing – something to which not a few have still failed to become accustomed. There are spectacular views of the beautiful theatre from the boxes in the adjoining *Theatre Museum (daily 9am–12.30pm and 1.30pm–5.30pm | 6 euros)*, which is full of memorabilia of all the famous prima donnas and composers. There are also tours of the stage workshops (see p. 46) in Tortona.

Weary tourists rest outside on the benches on the Piazza della Scala, under the thoughtful gaze of the omnipresent Leonardo da Vinci. The opposite side of the square belongs to the elegant *Palazzo Marino* (16th century), Milan's town hall since 1861. *Piazza della Scala | www.teatroallascala.org | Me-tro 1, 3 Duomo*

GARIBALDI, SEMPIONE & BRERA

Massive Sforza Castle watches over the entrance to the Parco Sempione, Milan's green oasis.

The Milanese visit the park to escape from the dust of the city and the air conditioning in their offices, to eat their

...nchtime salads, while the ladies kick off their high heels and stretch out their bare feet in the grass. And all the time, tourists are taking selfies inside and outside the castle. To the east of the castle is the district of Brera: the streets paved with river gravel surprise us with their original shops and pretty townhouses, while the area's flair is surpassed on the third Sunday of the month when the *Mercatino di Bera* spreads out its bric-a-bran and flowers over the Via Fiori Chiaria. The street cafés around the large Palazzo di Brera with the art academy and Pinacoteca, Milan's leading collection of art, are popular with students and staff of Corriere della Sera, Italy's biggest daily newspaper, which is based on the Via Solferino. The occasional ancient church kindles the curiosity, such as *San Simpliciano (Piazza San Simpliciano 7)*, from the early Middle Ages with two quiet cloisters. And like a mirage, the glazed high-rise buildings at the end of the Corso Garibaldi/Corso Como shopping district to the north of Brera tempt shoppers.

■1 CASTELLO SFORZESCO ★
(130 B2) (*ɱ J4*)

Strictly speaking, the castle is a fake. Large parts of it are actually (relatively) newly built, around 100 years old. Like the entrance tower: destroyed in the 16th century, it was rebuilt in 1900 to old drawings. Today, it most resembles the Renaissance residence of the 15th and 16th centuries, when the Sforza rulers practised their weaponry in the grounds and held glamorous celebrations in the ballrooms. These were also the Milan years of Leonardo da Vinci, at that time cultural and technical advisor to the dukes. Remains of some of his frescoes can still be seen on the walls. The Russians also liked the castle, and in fact the Kremlin in Moscow is based on it.

The medieval ruling family of the Viscontis built the first fortress here in the 14th century – but rather than to protect the city against enemies, it was to protect themselves from their subjects. And quite rightly so, because in 1447 it was stormed. In fact, the castle has even been used to fire at the Milanese, when the Austrians did so in the middle of the 19th century in the battles for national independence. It then remained a ruin for a long time, until 1900, when it was reconstructed with plenty of space for the city's art collections. Today the castle is an open, generous meeting place in the middle of the city. Stroll across the courtyards to the city park, and enjoy one of the open-air film showings or concerts.

There are guided tours on Saturdays *(2.30pm and 4pm)* and Sundays *(3pm)*; *(phone 0 26 59 69 37 to book | 10 euros)* of the crenellated battlements and underground chambers. On the inside, behind the parade ground, are the access points to the museum grounds (see following entry). *Admission free (museums 5 euros) | Piazza del Castello 3 | www.milanocastello.it | Metro 1, 2 Cairoli, Cadorna, Lanza*

■2 MUSEI DEL CASTELLO ●
(130 B1–2) (*ɱ J4*)

The range of the collections is tremendous: there are Lombardy sculptures from late antiquity to the Baroque, Northern Italian art from the early days to the 18th century, wall tapestries, furniture, musical instruments, weapons, ceramics and jewellery. If you can, spread your visit over several days. One of the highlights is Michelangelo's unfinished, moving sculpture INSIDER TIP "Pietà Rondanini", which the artist was still working on until a few days before his death in 1564. It has its own separate museum in

SIGHTSEEING IN GARIBALDI, SEMPIONE & BRERA

1 Castello Sforzesco

2 Musei del Castello

3 Parco Sempione

4 Pinacoteca di Brera

5 Porta Nuova

6 Studio Museo Achille Castiglioni

/// Pedestrian precinct

7 Torre Branca

8 Triennale Design Museum

the former Spanish hospital on the left-hand side of the parade ground. *Tue–Sun 9am–5.30pm | 5 euros | Piazza del Castello 3 | Metro 1, 2 Cairoli, Cadorna, Lanza*

3 PARCO SEMPIONE
(133 D–E 4–5) (∅ H–J 3–4)

A word of warning in advance: Milan has mosquitoes! You'll realise that at the test in this lovely nature park. Since 1893, it has covered 47 hectares at the back of the castle. Where the soldiers once learnt how to march and shoot, to-

the most romantic kissing scene in the history of art hangs here, "The Kiss", painted by Francesco Hayez in 1859. However, the fabulous Palazzo di Brera

Nicely run down – on the Piazza Gae Aulenti between the high-rise buildings of the Porta Nuova

day people work on the fitness course, and little Milanese learn how to ride their bicycles. There's romance on the charming bridges over the water lilies and ball-playing on the sports fields. The park is also home to the *Acquario (Tue–Sun 9am–1pm and 2pm–5.30pm | 6 euros | www.acquariocivicomilano.eu)* in a little Art Nouveau-style building of 1906 and the Arco della Pace, the "Arch of Peace" for Napoleon, now a popular meeting place for people on dates. The kiosks sell bibite and gelati. Access points to the park: Piazza Castello, Viale Alemagna, Piazza Sempione. *Daily 6.30am–8pm, March–Oct until 9/10/11.30pm | Metro 1, 2 Cairoli, Cadorna, Lanza*

▣ PINACOTECA DI BRERA ★
(131 D1) *(⑪ K4)*

Extra tutoring in kissing? Available in one of Italy's most significant art collections:

not only displays works of art, but also teaches how to paint them: since its opening at the beginning of the 19th century under Napoleon as an Institute of Fine Arts, the Pinacoteca has also been home to a renowned art academy.

Some of the highlights: in Room VI the moving "Pietà" by Giovanni Bellini (1455–60) and "The Dead Christ and Three Mourners", painted by Andrea Mantegna around 1478 with the "foreshortened Christ"; in Room XXIV "The Virgin with Child, Angels and Saints" by Piero della Francesca (1475) and "The Marriage of the Virgin" (1504) by Raffael. And in the courtyard, Napoleon triumphs as a naked ancient god – after all, we owe him a debt of gratitude for this fabulous "Institute of Fine Arts". The adjoining botanic gardens are perfect for relaxing. *Tue–Sun 8.30am–7.15pm (Thu until 10.15pm) | 10 euros | Via Brera 28 |*

pinacotecabrera.org | Metro 2, 3 Lanza, Monte Napoleone | tram 4, 12, 14

5 PORTA NUOVA (134 A2) (∅ K2)

Milan becomes vertical: from the short *Corso Como* fringed by bistros, a few nightclubs and boutiques, including Milan's loveliest Concept Store at no. 10, you'll come to the glazed high-rise enclave known as Porta Nuova. This is also where the ⚫ *Bosco Verticale*, the "vertical forest" grows, the two famous green residential towers. A lively, bustling area has developed at the foot of the towers on the central *Piazza Gae Aulenti* with cafés, stores and evening concerts. And you can see how new buildings are gradually advancing towards the neighbouring old working-class district of *Isola*. *Metro 2 Porta Garibaldi*

6 INSIDER TIP STUDIO MUSEO ACHILLE CASTIGLIONI (133 E5) (∅ H4)

Achille Castiglioni (1918–2002), one of the biggest names in Italian design, created a world-famous stool out of a tractor seat. You can follow his creative processes in his fascinating studio, which you can visit by appointment. *Tue-Fri 10am, 11am and noon, Thu also 6.30pm, 7.30pm, 8.30pm | 10 euros | Piazza Castello 27 | tel. 0 28 05 36 06 | www.achillecastiglioni.it | Metro 1, 2 Cadorna | Bus 57, 94*

7 TORRE BRANCA ★ ☼ (133 D5) (∅ H3)

The tower at the western entrance to the Parco Sempione, which was built to plans by the architect Giò Ponti, is exactly 109 m/358 ft high. It was sponsored by Branca, the well-known spirits company. There are fabulous views across the city from the look-out cabin – and guaranteed good weather, as otherwise the tower remains closed. Equally im-

pressive are the sea of lights that come on as evening descends. *Mid May–mid Sept Tue–Fri 3pm–7pm and 9.30pm–midnight, Wed also 10.30am–1.30pm, Sat/Sun 10.30am–2pm, 2.30pm–7.30pm and 8.30pm–midnight, mid Sept–mid May Wed 10.30am–12.30pm and 4pm–6.30pm, Sat 10.30am–1pm, 3pm–6.30pm and 8.30pm–midnight, Sun 10.30am–2pm and 2.30pm–7pm | 5 euros | Viale Alemagna/Parco Sempione | info about closures tel. 0 23 31 41 20 | Metro 1, 2 Cadorna | bus 61*

8 INSIDER TIP TRIENNALE DESIGN MUSEUM ⚫ (133 D5) (∅ H3–4)

Now, don't start asking questions, because we don't want to know what the gigantic floating duck thinks of the two naked men in the mysterious bathtub. The Bagni misteriosi fountain by the artist Giorgio De Chirico (1973) is part of the garden of the impressive 1930s Palazzo dell'Arte in the south-west part of the Parco Sempione. This is the site of the fabulous design museum with all the glorious Italian style creations and new shows, a meeting place for creative minds with cafés and a a panorama restaurant on the roof. *Tue–Sun 10.30am–8.30pm | 8 euros | Viale Emilio Alemagna 6 | www.triennaledesignmuseum.it | Metro 1 Cadorna | tram 1 | bus 61*

MAGENTA & SANT'AM-BROGIO

Milan's loveliest residential area – according to the people who live here – starts at the Corso Magenta, which heads west from the centre.

Stroll past impressive residences with roof gardens and meet the owners in one of Milan's oldest cafés, the *Pasticceria Marchesi (closed Mon | Via Santa Maria*

alla Porta 11a) right at the top of the Corso Magenta. As you wander along the streets, you'll keep coming across little groups of students from the Università Cattolica, hurrying from one lecture to the next in the palazzi scattered around Sant'Ambrogio. The quarter has plenty to offer – including a veritable highlight in the history of art: the "Last Supper" by Leonardo da Vinci.

■ CENACOLO VINCIANO ("LAST SUPPER") ★ (137 D1) (*Ø H4*)
To view Leonardo da Vinci's world famous masterpiece, you need to book well in advance (telephonic or via the internet). Then you will be allowed to enter the former refectory of the Dominican convent of Santa Maria delle Grazie for 15 minutes. For this painting (which took from 1495–97 to complete) da Vinci chose the moment during the last supper when Jesus predicts that one of his disciples will betray him. The Apostles, portrayed in groups of three, are all visibly shocked and dismayed.

Students at the university nearby aren't the only ones who appreciate the bars of the Corso Magenta

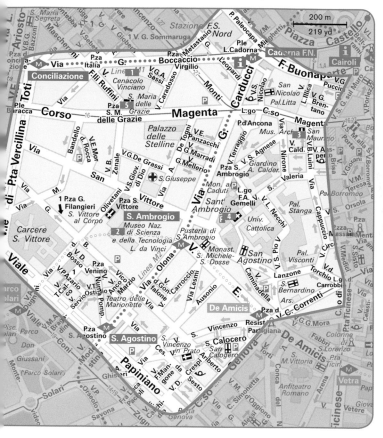

SIGHTSEEING IN MAGENTA & SANT'AMBROGIO

1 Cenacolo Vinciano ("Last Supper")

2 Museo Nazionale della Scienza e della Tecnologia Leonardo da Vinci

3 San Maurizio al Monastero Maggiore

4 Sant'Ambrogio

5 Santa Maria delle Grazie

This vast – 4.2 m/13.8 ft high and 9.1 m/ 29.9 ft wide – representation was a first for the artist (who had previously usually worked on small panels), and created as much of a stir in the art world as the screen did in the history of the cinema. The dramatic play of hands, the theatrical arrangement as if on a stage and the (now hardly reproducible) blending of colours, immediately made the painting famous. Even before da Vinci could complete the work, the first attempts at copies were circulated.

For aesthetic reasons, the artist chose to use tempera, which he applied to the dry plaster – and not the usual fresco technique where the paint is applied to a damp wall so that the colours could dry into the wall and last longer. As a result after only 20 years the painting was already damaged. Flooding and severe damage have caused restorers to be called in several times, sometimes with details such as beards or cloths being added. During the latest thorough restoration, lasting almost 20 years, the restorers tried to restore the painting, as far as possible, to its true original state – and removed all the false beards. *Tue–Sun 8.15am–6.45pm reservation mandatory tel. 02 92 80 03 60 | 12 euros | Piazza Santa Maria delle Grazie 2 | www.cenacolo vinciano.net | Metro 1, 2 Conciliazione, Cadorna | tram 16*

🟦 MUSEO NAZIONALE DELLA SCIENZA E DELLA TECNOLOGIA LEONARDO DA VINCI
(136–137 C–D2) *(㎡ H5)*

The 16th century Benedictine abbey eventually became a military barracks and then, in 1953, Italy's leading museum of technology and science with countless inventions that visitors are able to use interactively, including a number of projects by the science wizard Leonardo – and a real submarine. *Tue–Fri 9.30am–5pm, Sat/Sun 9.30am–6.30pm | 10 euros | Via San Vittore 21 | www.museoscienza.org | Metro 2 Sant'Ambrogio | bus 50, 58*

🟦 SAN MAURIZIO AL MONASTERO MAGGIORE (130 B3) *(㎡ J5)*

The interior of this charming Renaissance building (from 1503) was separated into a public part and a part for the cloistered Benedictine nuns. Both areas are now accessible and are decorated with **INSIDER TIP** *magnificent frescoes by Bernardino Luini* and his artists (1522–29). Regular concerts take place in the church and it also has the oldest organ in the city,

an Antegnati from 1554. The monastery area next door, has been converted into an *Archaeological Museum (Tue–Sun 9.30am–5.30pm | 5 euros)*. In the basement and the garden parts of the Roman city walls are still visible Along with Roman finds, including lovely mosaic floors that were partly unearthed when constructing the underground, a large model of the city illustrates just how impressive Milan was in Antiquity. *Corso Magenta 15 | Metro 1, 2 Cadorna | tram 16, 19*

🟦 SANT'AMBROGIO ★ ●
(130 A4) *(㎡ H5)*

You enter through the front portico, which is flanked by columns, and find yourself in a different world, in the holiest place in the city: the wonderfully atmospheric basilica, built in weathered brickwork. It was co-founded here by Ambrose of Trier, Bishop of Milan in the 4th century, and one of the fathers of Christianity in late Antiquity. The opera season at La Scala always begins on 7 December, the feast of St. Ambrose. Today's basilica dates back to the 12th/13th centuries. The precious gold altar depicts scenes from Ambrose's life, and the bishop is buried beneath it. You will find a mosaic portrait of him in the *San Vittore in Ciel d'Oro chapel (access to the right of the altar)*, made in 407 shortly after his death. It is probably exactly what he looked like – slender and serious. The cathedral treasure is housed next door. *Mon–Sat 7.30am–1.30pm and 2.30pm–7pm, Sun 7.30am–1.30pm and 3pm–7pm | Piazza Sant'Ambrogio 15 | Metro 2 Sant'Ambrogio | bus 58, 94*

🟦 SANTA MARIA DELLE GRAZIE
(137 D1) *(㎡ H4–5)*

The church is part of the Dominican convent next door, and its refectory is where Leonardo da Vinci painted his

The Renaissance dome of Santa Maria delle Grazie was started in 1492 by Donato Bramante

"Last Supper". It is evident from its appearance and elegance that it was a church for the upper classes rather than the people. Which it still is today; Milan's finest in the neighbourhood attend the Sunday service. It was none other than Donato Bramante (1444–1514), one of the greatest architects of the 15th century and the man who designed St. Peter's Basilica in Rome, who completed the church in 1492 (cupola, chancel and cloister) in the loveliest Renaissance style. The cloister, with the "frog fountain" and the flowering magnolias in spring, is a delightful haven of peace. There is another haven opposite, at the *Vigna di Leonardo* (see p. 86), a wine garden that is said to have belonged to Leonardo. *Piazza Santa Maria delle Grazie 2 | Metro 1, 2 Conciliazione, Cadorna | tram 16*

NAVIGLI & TORTONA

Who would have imagined that somewhere in the city was this tranquil canal idyll: people cycle and stroll along the banks of the canals, called the ★ navigli, and enjoy the culinary delights served at the street cafés.

Just picture it: for centuries, the city had a system of navigable and interconnected canals that were used to transport goods and people to Northern Italy and south to the Po, and thus as far as the Adriatic. All but two, the Naviglio Grande and the Naviglio Pavese, had disappeared by the beginning of the 20th century, the inner-city canals hidden under the asphalt. Tradesmen and boatmen initially lived in

45

low houses along the Navigli, but
...en the artists came and transformed
...he workshops in the courtyards into
their studios. A few of them still remain,
and on the first Sunday in May over 300
artists gather here to display their works
along the banks of the Naviglio Grande.
Today's creative minds – designers, fashion people, photographers, event plan-
ners – have made a home for themselves
in the neighbouring quarter of Tortona
just behind Porta Genova railway station,
which now includes the Museo delle Culture del Mondo, opened in 2015, and
several stylish hotels.

■ MUDEC & TORTONA

The Museo delle Culture del Mondo
(MUDEC) (136 B4) (*ω G7*) (Mon 2.30pm–
7.30pm, Tue, Wed, Fri, Sun 9.30am–
7.30pm, Thu, Sat 9.30am–10.30pm | Via
Tortona 56 | www.mudec.it) opened on
the site of the former Ansaldo locomotive factory in 2015, attracts you to the
neighbouring quarter of Tortona and
the Via Tortona and Via Savona. In the
rooms designed by the British star architect David Chipperfield, Milan checks
out the artworks of the big, wide world.
Find out more about the transformation
of this rough former labourers' quarter.
The *Scala Ansaldo Workshops (Via
Bergognone 34 | please phone 02 43
35 35 21 to book a guided tour)* for opera
performances at La Scala are also
housed on the Ansaldo site. The young
creative workshop *BASE* (base.milano.it)
has found its spectacular home here
and offers co-working, a hotel and a
café. Armani's fashion museum *Armani
Silos (Wed–Sun 11am–7pm | Via Bergog-
none 40)* is just opposite, and the head

Cafés and bars, night clubs and restaurants: the Navigli district is always lively, day and night

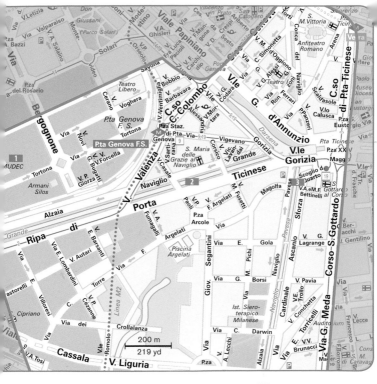

SIGHTSEEING IN NAVIGLI & TORTONA

1 MUDEC & Tortona   **2** Naviglio Grande

Pedestrian precinct

3 Naviglio Pavese & Darsena

office is next doors in a former chocolate factory. Via Tortona 27 is the home of the Superstudio (*www.superstudio group.com*), the address for design and fashion events. *Metro 2 Porta Genova | bus 68*

2 NAVIGLIO GRANDE
(136–137 A–D 4–5) (*🕮 C–H 7–8*)

Milan's "fun run": fine restaurants and trattoria, pubs and cocktail bars, ice cream parlours and sushi bars. On mild evenings, people wend their way amongst the tables and chairs along the

banks of the canal. The stands of the flea, antiques and clothing markets are set up on the last Sunday of the month, and hundreds of people gather on the banks of the Naviglio Grande, once the shipping connection to the Lago Maggiore. On summer weekends there are even *boat trips (www.naviglilombardi.it)*; go to the tourism office to find out more. Picturesque spots on the first section of the riverbank are the old laundry at the Vicolo dei Lavandai and the courtyard Cortile degli Artisti *(Alzaia Naviglio Grande 4)*. *Metro 2 Porta Genova | tram 2, 9*

3 NAVIGLIO PAVESE AND DARSENA
(137 D–E 4–6) (*Ø H7–8*)

At the first sight of the sun, people sit out on the terraces beside the Darsena and picnic on mozzarella, meat skewers or fish burgers – all culinary delights that you can buy from the food stands here or in the small market. Until just a few years ago it was a murky pond, full of rubbish, but the old harbour basin was refurbished in 2015 and, together with the adjoining Piazza XXIV Maggio – with the Porta Ticinese city gate of 1814 and two old customs stations – instantly became a popular meeting place. The rather quieter Naviglio Pavese, which links Milan to Pavia – now also with a cycle path – starts under the road bridge. *Metro 2 Porta Genova | tram 2, 9*

MORE SIGHTS

CASA MILAN & STADIO SAN SIRO

Some *tifosi* get tears in their eyes at the sight of the golden balls from the glorious days at the museum of the AC Milan, the *Casa Milan* (0) (*Ø E1*) (*daily 10am–7pm | 15 euros | Via Aldo Rossi 8 | casamilan.acmilan.com | Metro 5 Portello*). The museum is in Portello-City Life, a suburb that is full of interesting new buildings, and only a few Metro stations from the Stadio San Siro, the "Scala of football". A legend of modern spaciousness *(80,000 seats)*, the *Stadio Giuseppe Meazza* (0) (*Ø B2–3*) (*visits daily 9.30am–5pm except during matches and events | 17 euros | Via Piccolomini 5 | www.sansiro.net | Metro 5 San Siro Stadio | tram 16)*, opened in 1926, is named simply Stadio San Siro after the suburb.

INSIDER TIP CASA-MUSEO BOSCHI DI STEFANO ● (135 D3) (*Ø N2*)

This private museum is hidden away down a quiet residential street near the Corso Buenos Aires shopping street. There are hundreds of modern Italian works of art on the walls of the second-floor apartment, which is furnished with period furniture of the 1920s and 30s and was built by the then star architect Piero Portaluppi. *Tue–Sun 10am–6pm | admission free | Via Giorgio Jan 15 | www.fondazioneboschidistefano.it | Metro 1 Lima | tram 33 | bus 60*

INSIDER TIP CIMITERO MONUMENTALE
(133 D–E 1–2) (*Ø H–J1*)

Milan even has a town for its dead: the tombs with poignant tombstone sculptures and large family chapels in every imaginable architectural style make the Monumental Cemetery of 1866 a fascinating open-air museum. You may well be familiar with the names of some of the Milanese industrial families, such as Campari, Motta (panettone) and Pirelli (tyres). The great writer Alessandro Manzoni and the theatre producer and Nobel Prize winner Dario Fo (1926-2016) are buried in the *Famedio*, the "Hall of Fame". *Tue–Sun 8am–6pm | Piazzale Cimitero Monumentale | www.commune.milano.it/monementale | Metro 5 Monumentale | tram 9, 14*

GIARDINI PUBBLICI INDRO MONTANELLI (134 B–C 4–5) (*Ø L3–4*)

Next to the Parco Sempione is the second "green lung" in the centre. This is where you will find the Museo Civico di Storia Naturale and Planetarium (see "Travel with Kids"). The park continues along the Via Palestro to the south with the Neoclassical *Villa Reale*, home to the 19th century art collection, the *Galleria d'Arte Moderna* (GAM) (*Tue–Sun 9am–*

5.30pm, Thu until 10.30pm | 5 euros | www.gam-milano.com); modern art is on display in the former stables: *Padiglione d'Arte Contemporanea* (PAC) *(Tue–Sun 9.30am–7.30pm, Thu until 10.30pm | 8 euros | www.pacmilano.it). Access points: Via Manin, Via Palestro, Corso Venezia, Bastioni di Corso Venezia | Metro 1, 3 Palestro, Porta Venezia, Turati*

HANGAR BICOCCA ● (0) (*⊞ 0*)

The often monumental art of today is perfectly housed in these former factory halls in the former industrial quarter of Bicocca: for instance, the "Seven Heavenly Palaces" by the artist Anselm Kiefer, metal towers standing up to 27m high that were brought here in 2004. Since then the hangar, which is sponsored by the Pirelli tyre company, has been an exciting art space for artistic experimentation. Pleasant café-restaurant. *Thu–Sun 10am–10pm | admission free | Via Chiese 2 | www.hangarbicocca. org | bus 87, 728*

ISOLA (134 A–B 1–2) (*⊞ K–L1*)

Everyone wants to get to the "island", the labourers' quarter that was once cut off by railway tracks, and where the new high-rise buildings of the Porta Nuova are slowing encroaching behind Porta Garibaldi station. Around 21,000 people live here in vast blocks of flats from the turn of the 19th/20th century, but real estate prices are on the rise.

The identity of this district is still rather alternative: you'll find bars amongst coarse, graffiti-covered walls such as *Frida (Via Pollaiuolo 3)* with its "post-industrial" garden that you would think was in Berlin rather than Milan. Alternative creative shops are opening here, such as Algranti Lab *(Via Guglielmo Pepe 20–28)* with furniture made from recycled materials. And in the evening,

Lives by the tough contrast between old and new: the "in" district of Isola

people come to the "island" for a drink and to dine in the charming pubs and restaurants. *Metro 5 Isola*

MEMORIALE DELLA SHOAH (134 C1–2) (*⊞ M1*)

Hundreds of Milanese Jews were taken to concentration camps such as Auschwitz and Bergen-Belsen from Track 21. The memorial site on the east of the station building tells the story of this tragedy. *Mon 10am–7.30pm, Tue–Thu 10am–2.30pm, first Sunday of the month 10am–6pm | 10 euros | Piazza Edmond Jacob Safra | www.memorialeshoah.it | Metro 2, 3 Centrale*

FOOD & DRINK

A city that is always on the go won't slow down properly to eat. No sooner is one place popular than another one comes along to replace it.

While the luxury hotels compete against each other with their gourmet restaurants and people wait for Milan's star chef Carlo Cracco to open his new restaurant in the Galleria Vittorio Emanuele II, young people head off in a different direction and open their own establishments. Enjoyable and for every day, uncomplicated, but with selected quality products from Italian cuisine. Rather more all-day bistro or ristobar than restaurant, this concept is rapidly becoming something of a cult: the lifestyles of the customers and operators go together well. Food is the big topic, and there are

new food markets in the Galleria Vittorio Emanuele and in the harbour basin Darsena. Plus chic restaurants at the Museo del Novecento, the MUDEC, at the Triennale Design Museum.

If you don't want to spend too much, go to a pizzeria or one of the chains such as Panino Giusto with its delicious panini *(from 5 euros)* – the generous toppings are a meal in themselves. The branches on *Corso Porta Ticinese 1* or Piazza *XXIV Maggio 4* near the Porta Ticinese are more central *(more: www.paninogiusto. com)*; all are open daily from noon until 1 in the morning.

Princi (daily | www.princi.it) is the name of five stylish bakery cafés that serve focaccia, vegetable quiches and freshly-baked cakes, for instance in Brera at Lar-

Photo: Kitchen art at the Al Pont de Ferr

From risotto milanese to ethnic cuisine: culinary fashions also change quickly in Milan

go Foppa 2 or *Piazza XXV Aprile (more on the website)*. Very many modern bistros also cater to vegetarians and vegans. And the Milanese love sushi, as is evident from the many Japanese establishments.

Interesting, lively quarters with lots of restaurants and pubs are Navigli *(Via Cristoforo Colombo, Via Vigevano)*, around the Porta Ticinese *(Piazza Vetra)*, Brera, Isola *(Piazzale Carlo Archinto)*, the area around Corso Garibaldi/Corso Como plus Porta Romana and Porta Venezia.

There are places from every continent in the area around the *Viale Tunisia*. Many bars and restaurants close for two or three weeks in August. People have lunch between 12.30pm and 2.30pm, and dine in the evening between 7.30pm and 10.30pm, but food is available all day in many of the new bistros. The cover charge is also included on the bill, between 2 and 5 euros per person. Be sure to book in the more exclusive establishments, and if you really want to be safe, you'll do so in the more basic places, too.

BARS & CAFÉS

BAR BASSO (135 E4) ( N3)

This bar manages to stay popular with every generation, with fashion people and people in the neighbourhood. White-jacketed waiters serve cappuccino in the morning, sandwiches at lunch-

No prizes for guessing what is served as an aperitif at the *Camparino*

times, and towards evening *Negroni sbagliato*, the establishment's "in" aperitif. Not made with gin in the usual way, but as a lighter version that is mixed with spumante. And with it, rather than an all-you-can-eat buffet, it's more old-fashioned: olives and nuts. It's simply classy. *Closed Tue | Via Plinio 39 | www.barbasso.com | Metro 1 Lima | bus 60 | tram 33*

CAMPARINO IN GALLERIA ★
(131 D3) (K5)

On the first floor of the arcade, with the relaxed atmosphere of a club (except at lunchtime) with guests browsing newspapers, sipping Camparis or enjoying a cappuccino. You can also look down through the large windows and watch the goings-on in the Galleria. The bar on the ground floor is decorated with art nouveau mosaics. Living history: this is where Davide Campari first poured his aperitif in 1867. *Closed Mon | Galleria Vittorio Emanuele II | Piazza Duomo | Metro 1, 3 Duomo*

COVA (131 E3) (L4)

Elegant and traditional: homemade pastries have been sold here since 1817. A meeting place for customers of the exclusive fashion boutiques. *Closed Sun | Via Monte Napoleone 8 | Metro 1 San Babila*

GOD SAVE THE FOOD ●
(136 C4) (G7)

A large, bright all-day establishment in the designer quarter of Zona Tortona: café, ristorante, delicatessen, aperitif bar: a combination that you'll find more and more. *Daily | Via Tortona 34 | www.godsavethefood.it | Metro 2 Porta Genova*

LUCE (138 C6) (M8)

The retro pinball machine comes to life when you put a 100-lire coin in it, while old tearjerkers play free of charge on the jukebox. Cult film director Wes Anderson (Grand Hotel Budapest) created this café in the Prada Art Foundation with colourful wallpapers in the style of a 1950s department store. Everything's just right, whether panini or cocktails. *Closed Tue | Largo Isarco 2 | www.fondazioneprada.org | Metro 3 Lodi | bus 65*

INSIDER TIP **OTTO** (133 E3) *(⌖ J2)*

A large, relaxed drawing room on the lively Via Paolo Sarpi. Chinese immigrants have lived in this area on the Porta Volta for generations, but today it is being rediscovered by the Milanese. Get out your laptop while you have your caffelatte; also cake, drinks and free Internet. Some people come here to work, others to relax. Lovely soups at lunchtime, plus vegetable pies and salads, and music in the evenings. Sit on the large terrace surrounded by plants in summer. *Tue–Sun from 10am, Mon from 7pm | Via Paolo Sarpi 8 | www.sarpiotto.com | Metro 5 Monumentale | bus 94 | tram 2, 12*

INSIDER TIP **PAUSE** (135 D3) *(⌖ N2)*

With its vintage style and charming neighbourhood, this tiny café down a pretty side street of the Corso Buenos Aires could also be in Berlin. Many of the items on display in the café are for sale. *Daily | Via Federico Ozanam 7 | www.pausemilano.com | Metro 1 Lima*

PAVÉ ★ (134 C3) *(⌖ L2)*

Cakes not bombs: the motto of the group of youngsters that runs this easy-going café north-east of the Giardini Pubblici. A culinary hit is the oven-fresh Brioche 160%, called that because it is filled with loads of apricot jam. People queue for it at the weekends. The quiches served at lunchtime are also freshly baked. Make yourself comfortable at one of the large or small wooden tables, and enjoy the free Internet access. *Closed Mon | Via Felice Casati 27 | www.pavemilano.com | Metro 1, 3 Porta Venezia, Repubblica*

ICE CREAM PARLOURS

Ice cream parlours *(gelaterie)* are hugely popular in Milan; you'll find one on almost every street corner, and they are all quite rightly of very high quality. They are usually open from 11am–9pm or 11pm. One for all: *Pavé Gelati e Granite (Via Cesare Battisti 21 | Metro 1 San Babila)*

RESTAURANTS: EXPENSIVE

JOIA ★ (134 C4) *(⌖ L3)*

For years, chef Pietro Leemann has been proving in his quiet establishment that you can also create top cuisine using all-vegetarian ingredients. *Closed Sun | Via Panfilo Castaldi 18 | tel. 02 29 52 21 24 | www.joia.it | Metro 1 Porta Venezia*

AL PONT DE FERR (137 D5) *(⌖ H7)*

Close to the "Iron bridge" over the Naviglio Grande, this establishment looks like

★ **Camparino in Galleria**
To the bar where Campari was invented for a drink → p. 52

★ **Signor Vino**
Fabulous wines and specialities from all over Italy → p. 59

★ **Joia**
Haute cuisine doesn't have to include meat → p. 53

★ **Pavé**
People queue for the La 160% → p. 53

★ **Il Luogo di Aimo e Nadia**
One of Italy's top destinations for gourmets → p. 54

★ **Risotto Milanese**
A Milanese treat that you have to try – Ratanà serves one of the best → p. 57

MARCO POLO HIGHLIGHTS

a simple osteria with tables on the pavement. However, the food is fabulously creative and full of surprises. A little more basic: *Osteria Rebelot del Pont* right next door. *Daily | Ripa di Porta Ticinese 55 | tel. 02 89 40 62 77 | Metro 2 Porta Genova*

IL LUOGO DI AIMO E NADIA ★
(0) *(* *C6)*
For decades, this has been one of the top addresses for gourmets, and not only in Milan. Those who wish to experience *cucina italiana* with its authentic ingredients, typical combinations and cooking techniques on the very highest level would do well to head to this modern, elegant establishment. Even though it's hidden away in an anonymous area, away from the centre. *Closed Sat noon, Sun | Via Montecuccoli 6 | tel. 02 41 68 86 | www.aimoenadia.com | Metro 1 Primaticcio*

FAVOURITE EATERIES

Under the Sicilian sun
There are only a few seats at the small, warm ⊗ ★ *Pastamadre* (138 C4) *(* *M7) (Closed Sun | Via Bernardino Corio 8 | tel. 02 55 19 00 20 | Metro 3 Porta Romana | Budget–Moderate)* in the lively quarter of the Porta Romana. People sit on Spartan, recycled chairs and wait patiently for the delicious pasta made from organic flour that the Sicilian chef then finishes with sun-ripened tomatoes, sheep's cheese, juicy aubergines or sardine. Many people come again and again and know it's best to book in advance.

An old Lombardian trattoria
The venerable ★ *Osteria del Treno* (134 C3) *(* *L2) (Closed Sat noon and Sun noon | Via San Gregorio 46 | tel. 0 26 70 04 79 | www.osteriadeltreno.it | Metro 3 Repubblica | Moderate)* near the station, once the after-work choice of the railway workers, serves the kind of Lombardian recipes that are no longer found in many places. Pickled vegetables with first-class cheeses and hams, leek-stuffed dumplings, braised pork cheek, osso buco with semolina flan, all very carefully prepared with ⊗ slow-food products and served with a smile.

Eat, drink, shop
It's all well and good to let yourself be propelled along by the crowds on the Naviglio, but if you want to dine well and not like a tourist, better go around the corner to the Via Vigevano. The committed operators of the cosy, relaxed eatery *Taglio* (137 D4) *(* *H7) (Daily | Via Vigevano 10 | tel. 02 36 53 42 94 | www.taglio.me | Metro 2 Porta Genova | Moderate)* cook whatever the season gives them. Visitors can drink espresso or wine, chill out with culinary books, shop for culinary delights and dine well.

Turning old into hip
Moodily atmospheric, vintage Romanticism at the *Fonderie Milanesi* (137 F5) *(* *J7) (Closed Sun noon and Mon | Via Giovenale 7 | tel. 02 36 52 79 13 | bus 71, 79 | tram 9, 15 | Moderate)*: People meet for an aperitif, evening meal or brunch on Sundays at this fascinating labyrinth of abandoned factory halls and in the garden of an old foundry not far from the Porta Ticinese.

SETA MANDARIN ORIENTAL
(131 D2) (*[]] K4*)

In the competition for the best kitchen in Milan's luxury hotels, this one is well in the lead. Here at the Mandarin Oriental, the deluxe hotel between Brera and the fashion district Quadrilatero, everything is of the very best. Walk through the tasteful reception area, and you'll come to the elegant restaurant and lovely courtyard. A culinary journey of perfection starts with the best Mediterranean ingredients – and includes the perfect service, of course. *Daily | Via Andegari 9 | tel. 02 87 31 88 88 | www.mandarinorientaltal.it | Metro 3 Montenapoleone*

RESTAURANTS: MODERATE

EL BARBAPEDANA (137 D4) (*[]] H6*)

A small, cosy trattoria close to the Navigli that delights with its careful cuisine and traditional dishes such as risotto, *cotoletta* and *ossobuco*. Try their typical *nervetti*! Everything is delicious, the portion sizes generous. At the bottom end of the price category. *Closed Sun | Corso Cristoforo Colombo 7 | tel. 02 36 58 68 97 | www.elbarbapedana.it | Metro 2 Porta Genova | tram 2, 14*

BIOESSERI BRERA ⓥ (131 D1) (*[]] K3*)

Organic restaurants are opening up all over Milan. Like this friendly, modern bistro in the middle of Brera. You can start with breakfast, and the food continues until the evening, imaginatively prepared and made only from organic ingredients. Also popular with pure vegans. *Daily | Via Fatebenefratelli 2 | tel. 02 89 07 10 52 | www.bioesseri.it | Metro 3 Montenapoleone*

OSTERIA BRUNELLO (133 F3) (*[]] J2*)

In this lovely, modern trattoria in Brera, the menu and wine cellar offer fine Ital-

Simply irresistible: the Sicilian cuisine at the Pastamadre

ian classics such as tartar made from Piedmontese Fassona cattle or homemade ravioli stuffed with pumpkin. One highlight is the typical ● *cotoletta alla milanese*, a crispy cutlet fried with the bone in. Reasonable lunchtime prices! *Daily | Corso Giuseppe Garibaldi 117 | tel. 0 26 59 29 73 | www.osteriabrunello.it | Metro 2 Moscova*

LA DOGANA DEL BUONGUSTO
(137 E3) (*[]] J6*)

For once not modern and stylish, but pleasantly located within ancient walls, in the centre and close to the Basilica of San Lorenzo. Serves specialities from all over Italy: duck ham or burrata made from buffalo milk; risotto, of course; lamb and meat, and also freshwater fish in a green sauce and a memorable tiramisu. Prices on the lunchtime menu are moderate. Also has a wine bar *(closed lunchtime and Sun)*. *Closed Sat noon, Sun | Via Molino delle Armi 48 | tel. 02 83 24 24 44 | www.ladoganadelbuongusto.it | bus 93 | tram 3*

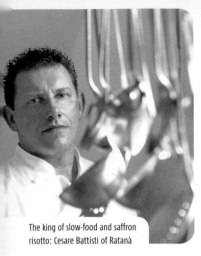

The king of slow-food and saffron risotto: Cesare Battisti of Ratanà

INSIDERTIP AL FRESCO
(136 B4) (*M G7*)

Literally in the open, because behind this charming country-style restaurant in the designer quarter of Tortona is an enchanting garden. The fresh, modern cuisine is the perfect match. *Closed Mon | Via Savona 50 | tel. 02 49 53 36 30 | www.alfrescomilano.it | Metro 2 Porta Genova | tram 14*

MERCATO DEL PESCE (134 C1) (*M M1*)

Milan may not be on the sea, but you can still get freshly-caught fish here. Standards here are so high that it is the first city to receive its supplies during the night. Fish goes straight from the stand into the pan on this fish market and restaurant left of the main station. Diners sit in elegance at all-white tables, and the presentation of the dishes is just as appetising. At the bottom end of the price category. *Closed Sun, Mon noon | Via Sammartini 70 | tel. 0 26 69 33 84 | Metro 3 Stazione Centrale*

PONTE ROSSO (137 D5) (*M H7*)

This friendly trattoria with the exquisite cuisine is a haven amongst the bustle on the Naviglio Grande; a delight where you can also sit outside in warm weather. *Closed Sun-evening | Ripa di Porta Ticinese 23 | tel. 0 28 37 31 32 | Metro 2 Porta Genova*

RATANÀ (134 A2) (*M K1*)

A Liberty-style villa behind the Porta Garibaldi railway station, in the midst of the new high-rises of the city: urbane simplicity on the inside, exclusive slow-

LEARN TO COOK ALLA MILANESE

Seeing all the wonderful displays in the delicatessens, will make you feel like cooking too. Several ● cooking schools offer courses that run for an evening or an afternoon – and in the kitchen people understand each other even without any knowledge of Italian. If you want to approach the business of cooking like a pro, then the cookery school of Italy's best gastro magazine, *La Cucina Italiana* (**133 D6**) (*M H4*) (*Piazzale Cadorna 5/Via San Nicolao 7 | tel. 02 49 74 80 04 | scuola. lacucinaita liana.it | Metro 1, 2 Cadorna*) is the answer, with plenty of courses on the finer points of antipasti, pasta, fish and desserts. Or perhaps you'd like to cook with friends and learn something as you go along? The passionate foodie *Clara Raimondi* (**132 B4**) (*M F3*) (*Piazza Febbraio 6 | tel. 33 58 05 98 52*) invites people into her home and cooks a multi-course lunch with them.

food ingredients and classics such as the sensational ★ Milanese saffron risotto or *ossobuco*. Carefully prepared dishes at affordable prices at lunchtime. A hit with its younger, chic clientèle. *Closed Sat/Sun in summer | Via Gaetano De Castilla 28 | tel. 02 87 12 88 55 | ratana.it | Metro 2 Porta Garibaldi*

A' RICCIONE DAL 1955 (0) (*m 0*)
A decidedly stylish restaurant that is popular with local connoisseurs (now updated, but founded in 1926) when they are in the mood for fresh oysters, for tender tuna or swordfish carpaccio, for spiny lobster from Sardinia, for red crayfish tails from Apulia, or for fish soup from the Adriatic. You can eat your way up one side of the "boot" and down the other on the best Italian fish fishes. *Closed Sut noon | Via Torquato Taramelli 70 | tel. 02 68 38 07 | www.ristorante ariccione.net | Metro 5 Marche*

SPAZIO ✄ (138 A1) (*m K1*)
Oh, to be a guinea pig here, for the students at Niko Romito's cookery school, the well-known celebrity chef from Abruzzo. They do a really good job. And where? On the third floor of the Galleria Vittorio Emanuele II, in a modern trattoria with views of the Galleria and the cathedral square. This is the *Mercato del Duomo*, in the right wing of the Galleria, where one food experience hotly pursues the next. *Daily | Via U. Foscolo 1 | tel. 02 87 84 00 | Metro 1 Duomo*

RESTAURANTS: BUDGET

ANCHE (133 F1) (*m K1*)
There are some very friendly places in the district of Isola behind the high-rise enclave Porta Nuova. This relaxed restaurant in a rustic vintage style has both, a bar *(daily 8pm–2am)* with cappuccinos and

cocktails, and a *restaurant* with tasty large and small dishes that you choose from a photo album. *Daily | Via Pastrengo/Via Carmagnola | tel. 33 18 22 40 02 | www.an che.it | Metro 2, 5 Stazione Porta Garibaldi*

INSIDER TIP ▶ ANTICA HOSTARIA DELLA LANTERNA (138 A4) (*m K6*)
You should be able to understand at least a little Italian, because there's no menu. The proprietor tells you what's on offer – although you can hardly go wrong with anything, as all the food is so good. Be sure to book! *Closed Sat for lunch and Sun | Via Mercalli 3 | tel. 02 58 30 96 04 | tram 15 | bus 94*

NERINO DIECI (137 F2) (*m J5*)
If you would like to dine here, be sure to book in advance. There is always a mad rush at this modern and appealing tratto-

LOW BUDGET

Follow the office workers during their lunch break to one of the affordable self-serve restaurants, such as the *Rita Moscova* **(134 B4)** (*m K–L3*) *(closed in evenings and Sat/Sun | Via della Moscova 3/Via Turati | Metro 3 Turati)* near the Giardini Pubblici.

Many sophisticated upmarket restaurants offer inexpensive dishes during *pausa pranzo* or lunch break.

Fresh drinking water, controlled and free: there are around 450 water dispensers, called *draghi verdi* (green dragons), all over the city area – to find out just where they are, consult the map at *www.fontanelle.org* (tab „Mappa fontanelle").

LOCAL SPECIALITIES

bresaola – dried beef, cut in paper thin slices

busecca – tripe stew with beans

cassoeula – pork stew with sausage and cabbage

co(s)toletta milanese – crumbed veal, either a cutlet or escalope

gnervitt (nervetti) – pressed beef cartilage with oil, vinegar and onions, a typical antipasto

grana – Lombard variant of parmigiano cheese

gremolata – spicy sauce with herbs, garlic and lemon zest, often served with ossobuco

ossobuco – slices of veal shank braised with vegetables (photo right)

panettone – a light Christmas sweet bread with raisins and candied orange

(pesce) persico – perch, e.g. deep-fried, speciality of Lake Como

pizzoccheri – short buckweed ribbon noodles served with Savoy cabbage and potatoes, speciality of Valtellina

risotto milanese – rice, sautéed with onions and butter and simmered with saffron and stock, served sprinkled with Parmesan (photo left)

taleggio – an aromatic soft cheese from the Lombardy mountains

tortelli di zucca – small pasta pockets filled with pumpkin, a speciality of Mantua

zuppa pavese – meat broth with a piece of toast topped with a poached egg

ria in the middle of Milan. You'll see why as soon as you get there: the atmosphere is friendly, the food fresh, simple and yet varied. The chef loves fish – and everything else as well. And there's an excellent lunch offer for between 9 and 12 euros. *Closed Sat noon, Sun | Via Nerino 10 | tel. 02 39 83 10 19 | Metro 1 Duomo | tram 2, 14*

PIZ (137 F2) (*Ø K5*)

Only three types of pizza are served at this small, colourful pizzeria that is al-

ways full: fragrant, delicious, and the perfect fortification in this central shopping district. *Closed Sun and Mon lunchtime | Via Torino 34 | tel. 02 86 45 34 82 | Metro 1 Duomo | tram 2, 14*

SAPORI SOLARI (0) (*Ø D5*)

It's a bit of a way to this land of milk and honey – oops; make that ham and cheese – but it's worth it: you can buy the tasty products or enjoy them sitting at rustic tables in the shop. It's always full, so be sure to book in advance! *Closed Sun | Via Anguissola 54 | tel. 02 36 51 38 16 | Metro 1 Piazzale Bande Nere*

SIGNOR VINO ⭐ (131 E4) (*ΩΩ K5*)

This impressive wine store behind the cathedral's apse demonstrates what Italy's vineyards have to offer. Choose from the menu, which is organised by region – reasonable prices for the location. *Daily | Piazza Dumo/corner Corso Vittorio Emanuele II | tel. 02 89 09 25 39 | www. signorvino.it | Metro 1, 3 Duomo*

INSIDER TIP UPCYCLE MILANO BIKE CAFÉ (135 F6) (*ΩΩ O2*)

The keen cyclists of the founding group have turned this bike repair shop into an ultra-cosy café, a cult among the students of the Città Studi campus. Visitors sit in beach chairs or at long communal tables to surf, drink fresh juices, good beers and cocktails; the menu includes vegan choices, juicy burgers and smoked fish. Occasionally live concerts. *Daily | Via A.M. Ampère 59 | tel. 02 83 42 82 68 | www.upcyclecafe.it | Metro 2 Piola*

INTERNATIONAL CUISINE

RAVIOLERIA (133 D3) (*ΩΩ H2*)

A street food kiosk in the Chinese quarter where people wait in line to be served. The offer includes steamed Chinese dumplings stuffed with meat from the butcher's next door or with organic vegetables. Once served, people sit on the nearest street bench to enjoy their food. *Daily | Via Paolo Sarpi 27 | Metro 5 Monumentale | bus 94 | tram 2, 12*

WARSÀ (135 D4–5) (*ΩΩ M3*)

A number of good Ethiopian or Eritrean restaurants testify to the fact that for generations, immigrants from the former Italian colony on Africa's Cape Horn have settled in Milan. Pleasant atmosphere, typical music. *Closed Wed | Via Melzo 16 | tel. 02 20 16 73 | www. ristorantewarsa.it | Metro 1 Porta Venezia | Budget–Moderate*

ZAZÀ RAMEN (133 F4) (*ΩΩ K3*)

The Milanese find Japanese cuisine elegant; it suits them. Accordingly, there are lots of Japanese restaurants, including some fine ones. This one here in Brera is light, uncomplicated and specialises in ramen, the Japanese wheat noodles that are consumed in soups with meat, fish and vegetables. *Daily | Via Solferino 48 | tel. 02 36 79 90 00 | www.zazaramen.it | Metro 2 Moscova*

Eritrea in Milan: Warsà

SHOPPING

CITY ▸ WHERE TO START?

From the cathedral square, head to the **Galleria Vittorio Emanuele II (131 D3)** (*⬚ K5*) or the **Corso Vittorio Emanuele II** and the luxury department stores La Rinascente and Excelsior. About 600 m/2000 ft up the Corso you'll come to the **Quadrilatero della Moda (131 E–F 2–3)** (*⬚ K–L4*). Other shopping areas, including several for younger shoppers, are **Via Dante (130 C3)** (*⬚ J4–5)* towards the castle, **Via Torino (130 C4–5)** (*⬚ J–K5*) towards the Porta Ticinese, **Corso Vercelli (136 A–B1)** (*⬚ F–G 4–5)* in the east and west of the **Corso Buenos Aires (134–135 C–E 2–4)** (*⬚ M–N 1–3)*.

When it comes to shopping, Milan has an irresistible pull. Expectations are high, but the city accepts that with equanimity. As the capital of fashion, design and delicatessen, it is well equipped for anything.

There's more than the up-market department stores, the luxury boutiques of Italian and international fashion labels, and all the global market chains. Whatever people want, they'll find it: the latest trends alternate with vintage, glamorous, classic and crazy, markets and outlets. If you come in January or July/August, you'll be there for the *saldi*, when prices tumble by between 30 and 50 percent. What has made the city's name for its shopping is the ★ *Quadrilatero della Moda*, the

In a city of fashion and design: slip into some haute couture – shopping in Milan is simply a lot of fun

„Square of Fashion". Not even New York has so many boutiques where the world's best fashion creators present their wares with style and elegance on such a small space. The best-known street is the Via Monte Napoleone. The luxurious sights continue on the tranquil parallel street, Via della Spiga. One other highlight is Armani's elegant store on the Via Manzoni.

You'll find shopping areas around the Corso Vittorio Emanuele II between the cathedral and San Babila, on the Via Torino and further along on the Corso di Porta Ticinese, at the Corso Buenos Aires between the Porta Venezia and Piazzale Loreto, and on the Corso Vercelli. Art, curiosities and antiques are on offer in the Brera quarter and around the Corso Garibaldi/Corso Como.

Milan only shuts down three times during the year: on the days around Ferragosto (15 August) when all of Italy flocks to the beaches, as well as on the 7th/8th December and on Christmas. Shops are open until 7.30/8pm (some-

ANTIQUES & ANTIQUARIANS

Whether fine or hearty: everything the Italians need for food is available at Eataly

times even longer). On Sundays only the shops in the city centre are open and on Monday mornings many keep their shutters down. Department stores and supermarkets are open throughout the day (orario continuato) but the retail trade close for lunch between 12.30pm or 1pm until 3.30pm or 4pm.

ANTIQUES & ANTIQUARIANS

ANTICHI VIZI (130 C2) (*∅ K4*)
Chamber of wonders – or of horrors: anatomy models, wolves' sculls that have bleached to sculptures, curious display cabinets, strange dolls – many of the items are old and artistic. *Via dell'Orso 12 | www.antichivizi.com | Metro 3 Napoleone | bus 61*

SISTERS' ANTIQUES (130 B3) (*∅ J5*)
A treasure trove for lovers of beautiful old jewellery: brooches and necklaces from the Empire era or in the art nouveau style, Russian Fabergé objects, costume jewellery from the 1940s and more. *Via San Giovanni sul Muro 18 | Metro 1 Cairoli | tram 16*

BOOKS, CDS & FILMS

BIRDLAND (130 C6) (*∅ J6*)
A treasure trove for music lovers with a preference for jazz, blues, modern sounds, and a large range of scores and musical films. *Via Vettabbia 9 | www.birdlandjazz.it | Metro 3 Missori | bus 94*

BOCCA 1773 (131 D3) (*∅ K5*)
This is one of the oldest shops in the city, built even before the Galleria, an art book store of the very finest. *Galleria Vittorio Emanuele II 12 | www.libreriabocca. com | Metro 1, 3 Duomo*

FELTRINELLI
This is the largest Italian bookstore chain and they have numerous branches in Milan, such as the on the cathedral square in the basement of the Galleria Vittorio Emanuele II (131 D3) (*∅ K5*) (*Mon–Sat*

10am–11pm, Sun 10am–8pm | www.lafel trinelli.it | Metro 1, 3 Duomo) which, together with Ricordi CDs (sheet music too), covers over a total area 43,000 ft². On the *Piazza Cavour* (127 E1) (*🛍 L3–4*) you will find the branch of Feltrinelli International *(Mon–Sat 9am–7.30pm | www.lafeltrinelli.it | Metro M 3 Turati, tram 2)* with foreign language titles and international press.The branches at the station and on the *Via Manzoni 12* (131 D2) (*🛍 K4*) *(Mon–Sat 6am–7.30pm, Sun 7am–1.30pm | Metro 3 Monte Napoleone)* also stock foreign-language titles and international press.

DELICATESSEN & WINE

CAMINADELLA DOLCI (130 A5) (*🛍 H6*)
Cakes in all sizes, biscuits, colourful macarons, vegetable quiches – all of this in a pretty shop and café tucked away in a courtyard. *Via Caminadella 23 | Metro 2 Sant'Ambrogio | tram 2, 14*

CIOCCOLATITALIANI (137 E3) (*🛍 H–J6*)
This place is all about chocolate, from fabulous chocolate espresso to fabulous ice cream – a very successful Milanese chain. *Via Edmondo De Amicis 25 | www.cioccolati taliani.it | Metro 2 Sant'Ambrogio*

COTTI (134 A3) (*🛍 K2*)
A traditional establishment with around 1000 Italian wines. Next to the shop is a small bar that serves a selection of some of the wines. *Closed Sun/Mon | Via Solferino 42 | Metro 2 Moscova*

INSIDER TIP **DOLCEMENTE**
(133 F3) (*🛍 J2–3*)
The cult address for dessert artists: you'll find all the equipment for designer cakes and the ingredients for patisserie and confectionery here, such as icings, sugar flowers, natural colourings and so on. *Via*

Alessandro Volta 6 | www.dolcemente web.com | Metro 2 Moscova

EATALY SMERALDO ⭐
(133 F3) (*🛍 K2*)
The quality delicacies all over Italy in this highly renowned chain, a veritable paradise for foodies, have found the appropri-

---

⭐ **Quadrilatero della Moda**
The chic fashion district
→ **p. 60**

⭐ **Rossana Orlandi**
You can count on the owner's unique style, a blend of contemporary and vintage items
→ **p. 65**

⭐ **Peck**
Where Milan shops for their culinary delights → **p. 64**

⭐ **Artemide**
For the loveliest light fittings in town → **p. 64**

⭐ **Armani**
The store for absolute elegance
→ **p. 66**

⭐ **La Rinascente**
A department store with eight floors of style → **p. 66**

⭐ **Mercatone del Naviglio Grande**
Antiques and flea market on the banks of the canal → **p. 68**

⭐ **Eataly Smeraldo**
Affordable Italian culinaria: an excellent concept store for foodies → **p. 63**

MARCO POLO HIGHLIGHTS

ate setting in a former theatre close to the Corso Como. The store contains bistros, bars and the gourmet eatery Alice. There is also a branch of Eataly in the Coin department store at Piazza 5 Giornate. *Piazza XXV Aprile | Metro 2 Porta Garibaldi*

ERNST K KNAM (139 D2) (*M6*)
In 1992, Ernst Friedrich Knam opened his pasticceria in Milan. Since then he has established himself here as the „King of Chocolate" with his wonderful chocolate creations, his cakes and gateaux at every imaginable price. *Via Augusto Anfossi 10 | www.eknam.com | tram 9*

ESSELUNGA (134 A3) (*K2*)
There is a branch of Italy's top supermarket chain under the Piazza Gae Aulenti between the high-rises of Porta Nuova. *Viale Don Luigi Sturzo 13 | Metro 2 Porta Garibaldi*

PECK ★ (130 C4) (*K5*)
A revelation in gastronomy over several floors: pasta and cheese, jams and wine, fruit and meat, the exotic and the unusual. If you have not been to Peck, you do not know Milan. *Via Spadari 9 | www. peck.it | Metro 1, 3 Duomo*

DESIGN & LIFESTYLE

ARTEMIDE ★ (131 F3) (*L4*)
Arco is the light that arches over the table, tolomeo the classic desk lamp: you'll find all the lights and lamps by the masters such as Ettore Sottsass, Gae Aulenti, Vico Magistretti and Michele de Lucchi, to name but a few, here. *Corso Monforte 19 | Metro 1 San Babila*

BIALETTI (131 D4) (*K5*)
Italy's best-known brand for fine kitchen accessories, in particular its „Moka" for making espresso, is unbeatable in form and quality. *Piazza dei Mercanti 7 | www. bialetti.it | Metro 1, 3 Duomo*

CARGO HIGH TECH (133 F3) (*K2*)
This mega store with its hotchpotch of stylish, unusual, shabby-chic, folkloristic and elegant objects for home, kitchen and garden is housed in a former ink factory. With furniture, clothing, writing utensils, fragrances and much more. *Closed Mon | Piazza XXV Aprile 12 | www. cargomilano.it | Metro 2 Porta Garibaldi*

10 CORSO COMO (133 F3) (*K2*)
In this lifestyle emporium, the tastes of the owner, Carla Sozzani, defines the

CHINATOWN ALL'ITALIANA

They sell towels and toys at the main station, in the Galleria or on the cathedral square: there are around 27,000 Chinese here and they also give Milan a far-eastern culinary flair. During the 1920s the first Chinese traders settled in this cosmopolitan city. As they settled, one relative brought the next along and one family the next family.

And they kept coming. Most of them live around the Via Paolo Sarpi, full of Chinese shop signs and today a pleasant stroll between the Parco Sempione and the Monumental Cemetery. The Chinese shopping centre *The Oriental Mall* **(133 D3)** (*H2*) *(Tram 12, 14)* sells high-tech, cheap stuff, but also Asian quality products and foods.

Cool, cooler, 10 Corso Como: this emporium of style isn't a shop – it's a complete work of art

range – which is exquisite, cool and playful at the same time. In her fashion space, she collects what she likes best as well as lesser known designers, for men and women, also accessories from bags to umbrellas and notebooks. Even the interior is decorated with all sorts of original design objects. There is also an art gallery on the upper floor with photo exhibitions and an art bookshop. You can even live their chic lifestyle in three B&B suites *(www.3rooms-10corsocomo. com | Expensive)*. They're a little pricey, but the bathrooms alone will fill you with inspiration for your next DIY project at home … The café-restaurant with an extremely sophisticated cuisine in the charmingly landscaped courtyard is open until 1am. *Corso Como 10 | www.10corsocomo.com | Metro 2 Porta Garibaldi*

INSIDER TIP **MARIO LUCA GIUSTI**
(130 C1) (*ω J2*)
The trendy jugs in „synthetic crystal" – acrylic – by the Florentine designer are ultra-light, colourful and virtually unbreakable. *Via Garibaldi 12 | Metro 2 Lanza*

MORONI GOMMA (131 E3) (*ω L4*)
Made from rubber, plastic, card and lightweight metal: weird and useful, objects, furniture, equipment, and accessories. *Corso Giacomo Matteotti 14 | www.moronigomma.it | Metro 1 San Babila*

ROSSANA ORLANDI ★ (136 C2) (*ω G5*)
This shoppers' paradise is in an old tie factory tucked away in a lovely backyard (you have to ring the bell) with selected furnishings, crockery, objects from design talents in the Netherlands, Scandinavia, Italy. A real treasure trove! *Via*

Matteo Bandello 14/16 | Metro 2 Sant'Ambrogio

GIFTS, THIS & THAT

FOTO VENETA OTTICA (130 B5) (*ⓂJ5*)
Go up to the first floor in this eyewear shop, which has a INSIDER**TIP** fabulous range of vintage eyewear frames, sunglasses from the 60s, and ski goggles from the 70s. The third generation of this family of opticians are enthusiastic collectors, and have accumulated a great diversity of unique objects. *Via Torino 57 | www.fotovenetaottica.com | tram 2, 3, 14*

LISA CORTI HOME TEXTIL
(134 C4) (*ⓂM3*)
Lisa Corti presents her delightfully cheerful fabric creations in this lovely shop, inspired by the colours and woven fabrics of Africa and India, places that she has been travelling to since she was a child. *Via Lecco 2 | www.lisacorti.it | Metro 1 Porta Venezia | tram 9*

COLTELLERIA LORENZI (130 B3) (*ⓂJ5*)
Oyster knives, nail brushes, mocha machines, Parmesan graters and shaving brushes are only a few of the elegant accessories available from this 100-year-old shop. *Corso Magenta 1 | www.o-lorenzi.it | tram 12, 14 | Metro 2 Cadorna*

INSIDER**TIP** PETTINAROLI
(131 D3) (*ⓂK4*)
Historical street and topographical maps – this has been the Milanese address for stylish letters and calling cards since 1881. *Piazza San Fedele 2/entrance Via T. Marino | Metro 1, 3 Duomo*

DEPARTMENT STORES

ARMANI ★ (131 E2) (*ⓂK4*)
A very special kind of department store and the world of Giorgio Armani, Italy's most famous fashion designer: his creations are presented on the various floors, and there is also a café, a restaurant, an art book shop and the elegant sushi restaurant *Nobu*, plus a luxurious hotel on the roof. *Via Alessandro Manzoni 31 | Metro 3 Monte Napoleone*

THE BRIAN & BARRY BUILDING
(131 F3) (*ⓂL5*)
It might sound very British, but behind it are the Zaccardi brothers from Monza, well-known gentlemen's outfitters and today the owners of this extremely elegant mega store with 12 floors of ladies' and men's fashions ranging from street wear to classic, plus shoes, jewellery, cosmetics and, of course food, and the gourmet restaurant *Asola*. *Via Durini 28 | thebrianebarrybuilding.it | Metro 1 San Babila*

COIN
(139 D2) (*ⓂM5*)
The flagship store of this long-established, elegant department store consists of seven floors. One of its particular attractions is the extensive interior design range, another the Happy Hour at the ☆ *Globe* panoramic restaurant. *Piazza 5 Giornate 1a | tram 9,12*

EXCELSIOR MILANO ●
(131 E3) (*ⓂL5*)
An old city cinema that has been converted into a fashion, food and design emporium – an addition to the many luxury establishments. *Galleria del Corso 4 | Metro 1, 3 Duomo*

LA RINASCENTE ★
(131 E3) (*ⓂK5*)
Luxury department store spanning seven floors with brunch restaurant and a bar on the roof (☆ terrace facing towards

the cathedral). Clothing, perfume, accessories and designer household wares. *Via Santa Radegonda 3/ Piazza Duomo | Metro 1, 3 Duomo*

CLOTHING & ACCESSORIES

INSIDER TIP ASAP – AS SUSTAINABLE AS POSSIBLE

This label tailors fashions of a clever simplicity made in quality materials and models from the previous season. *Corso Garibaldi 100 | www.asaplab.it | Metro 2 Moscova*

BOGGI
(131 F3) (*L4–5*)

Gentlemen's outfitter, popular with young men as well for its well-tailored shirts, jeans and short coats. Excellent value for money. Eight branches in the city, e.g.: *Piazza San Babila 3 | Metro 1 San Babila*

ES: IL BELLO DELL'INTIMO
(130 B3) (*J4*)

Stunning lingerie and swimwear by exclusive Italian labels with their feminine – sometimes glamorous, sometimes girly – creations. They even have outfits for beach parties. *Foro Bonaparte 71 | Metro 1 Cairoli | tram 1, 4*

IL GUFO
(131 E3) (*L5*)

You can buy lovely children's clothes in Milan, and the ones by this specialist label are ultra-cute. *Via San Pietro all'Orto 22 | www.ilgufo.it | Metro 1 San Babila*

INSIDER TIP NO. 30 MILANO
(131 E2) (*L4*)

Ladies' and men's fashions from a rear building off the smart shopping street. An excellent range, including interesting niche labels, and extremely friendly assistance. *Via della Spiga 30 | www.n30milano.com | Metro 3 Monte Napoleone*

OFFICINA SLOWEAR
(133 F4) (*K3*)

For favourite items that are to last a long time: excellently made casual fashions for men. *Via Solferino 18 | www.slowear.com | Metro 2 Moscova | tram 12*

PIUMELLI
(133 D3) (*K5*)

Fine leather gloves in every possible colour – once a glove maker from Naples, today a cult brand (also a shop in the Via Monte Napoleone 18). *Galleria Vittorio Emanuele II | www.piumelli.com | Metro 1, 3 Duomo*

LOW BUDGET

The good brands and prices at Milan's first fashion outlet in a backyard remain unsurpassed: Il Salvagente **(139 E1) (*N5*)** (*Via Fratelli Bronzetti 16 | www.salvagentemilano.it | tram 12 | bus 60, 73, 93*).

In the middle of Quadrilatero are two designer fashion outlets of DMAG: at Via Bigli 4 *(www.dmag.eu)* and at Via Manzoni 44, both **(131 E2) (*K4*)**.

The Saturday flea market Fiera di Sinigaglia **(136 C4–5) (*G–H7*)** *(8am–6pm | Alzaia Naviglio Grande/ corner Via Valenza | www.fieradisiniaglia.it | Metro 2 Porta Genova | tram 2)* sells clothing, shoes and accessories at good prices. The where and when of the many weekly markets: *mercati-settimanali.it/Milano*

VINTAGE CAVALLI E NASTRI
(130 B5) (⬦ J6)
Second-hand at the highest quality, from Prada and Dior, especially from the 1970s. There's a second shop in Via Brera 2. *Via Gian Giacomo Mora 3 | www.cavallienastri.com | Metro 2 Sant'Ambrogio*

WAIT AND SEE (130 C4) (⬦ J5)
Unusual bags and accessories, eccentric designer pieces, dresses – a treasure trove of original finds, and in a central yet concealed spot that is full of flair. *Via Santa Marta 14 | Metro 1, 3 Duomo*

WOK (137 F4) (⬦ J7)
A boutique with exclusive street wear, selected items by international labels that are turning to new high-tech materials. *Viale Col di Lana 5 | www.wok-store.it | tram 3, 9, 15*

COSMETICS

DIEGO DALLA PALMA ●
(130 C2) (⬦ J4)
Come and be made up, styled and advised by Milan's make-up guru and his crew. To make an appointment: tel. 02 87 68 18. *Via Madonnina 15 | www.diegodallapalma.com | Metro 2 Lanza*

PROFUMO (133 F5) (⬦ K4)
Good advice and unusual fragrances in this lovely shop in Brera. You're sure to find the fragrance for you. *Via Brera 6 | Metro 2 Lanza | bus 61*

MARKETS

INSIDER TIP EAST MARKET MILANO
(0) (⬦ Q2)
Don't worry, there's no rubbish from the cellar. Instead, private individuals sell and exchange the things they no longer need or want in this hall in Lambrate:

clothing, books, vinyls, collections. Food and music ensure it's a cool event. See Facebook or the website for the dates. *Via Privata Giovanni Ventura 14 | Metro 2 Lambrate | bus 82*

MERCATO DELLA TERRA ⬦
(133 D2) (⬦ H2)
Slow-food and farmers' markets on the first and third Sundays of the month on the Fabbrica del Vapore, a cultural centre on the site of a former factory. *Via Giulio Cesare Procaccini 4 | tram 12, 14 | bus 37*

MERCATO DI VIALE PAPINIANO
(136–137 C–D3) (⬦ G–H6)
The biggest weekly market in the centre, with food, clothing, shoes and household goods. *Tue 7.30am–2pm, Sat 7.30am–6pm | Viale Papiniano | Metro 2 Sant'Agostino | tram 2, 14*

MERCATONE DEL NAVIGLIO GRANDE ★ (137 D4–5) (⬦ G–H7)
The popular market for antiques and bric-a-brac is in an atmospheric location on the banks of the Naviglio Grande. On the last Sunday of the month (except in July and August). *Alzaia Naviglio Grande 4/ Ripa di Porta Ticinese | Metro 2 Porta Genova*

JEWELLERY

DONATELLA PELLINI ⬦
(130 A–B3) (⬦ J5)
Glamorous jewellery made from synthetic resin and semi-precious stones; also has its own eco line. Branches: *Via Manzoni 20 and Via Morigi 9. Corso Magenta 11 | www.pellini.it | Metro 1, 2 Cadorna*

PILGIÒ (130 A5) (⬦ H5–6)
Antonio Piluso's unconventional creations in gold, terracotta, wood and iron – archaic and modern at the same time.

Via Caminadella 6 | www.pilgio.com | Metro 2 Sant'Ambrogio

SHOES

ANTONIA (130 C2) (*ⅉ J4*)

Antonia Giacinti is widely regarded as a top buyer, and proves her skills in her lovely multi-brand store in Brera in the

well the ladies of Milan are able to walk in them! *Via Statuto 4 | Metro 2 Moscova | tram 2, 12, 14 | bus 43, 94*

BAGS & CASES

BRACCIALINI (131 F3) (*ⅉ L4*)

The Florentine brand offers beautifully made leather bags that are styled and

Lovers of the unusual will think they've gone to heaven: the Mercatone del Naviglio Grande

Palazzo Cagnola not only in the clothing she selects, but also with the fabulous shoes and trainers. *Via Cusani 5 | Metro 2 Lanza | bus 61*

INSIDER TIP BELFIORE (132 B6) (*ⅉ F4*)

Home-made moccasins and elegant, classic lace-ups at surprisingly affordable prices – since 1953. *Via Belfiore 9 | Metro M 1 Wagner*

LA VETRINA DI BERYL
(133 F4) (*ⅉ J–K3*)

Carrie Bradshaw would have loved these original heels – and it's amazing how

decorated with tremendous humour. *Via della Spiga 5 | Metro 3 Monte Napoleone*

MH WAY (138 B1) (*ⅉ L5*)

Makio Hasuike's plastic briefcases, backpacks, bags for notebooks and iPads – cool but amusing. *Via Durini 2 | www. mhway.it | Metro 1 San Babila*

INSIDER TIP VALEXTRA (131 D2) (*ⅉ K4*)

Italy's most elegant suitcase manufacturer. Beautiful objects at the corresponding prices. *Via Alessandro Manzoni 3 | www. valextra.it | Metro 3 Monte Napoleone*

ENTERTAINMENT

CITY **WHERE TO START?**

Post-aperitif the Milanese head out to areas such as the **Corso Sempione (132–133 C–D4)** (*⌖ G–H3*) with its meeting spot at Arco della Pace because everything is close there. The venues around the **Porta Ticinese (137 E4)** (*⌖ J7*) and the **Parco delle Basiliche (137 E3–4)** (*⌖ J6*) have a more relaxed atmosphere.

Another popular area is around the **Corso Como (133 F2–3)** (*⌖ K2*) which also has some good nightspots but the **Naviglio Grande (136–137 A–D 4–5)** (*⌖ C–H 7–8*) offers something for everyone!

If you think that this city ever rests, you are mistaken. During the day, people work and money is earned and in the evenings they relax in a bar or let off steam in a club.

With the world famous La Scala as well as a concert and theatre programme unmatched anywhere else in Italy, Milan consolidates its reputation as the cultural capital of the country every day. Milan is also the city of the aperitif, of Happy Hour that starts at 6pm and goes on until 9pm – with finger food buffets that can easily replace the evening meal. It's a good idea to book in advance. The discos that have a restaurant also start the evening with the aperitif buffet. Just how well food and pleasure go together is demonstrated by the suc-

Grand opera and the Piccolo Teatro: at night people do not switch off, they just switch over – to all sorts of entertainment

cess of the meeting places on the Corso Sempione or Corso Como in Isola north of the Porta Garibaldi railway station, in Porta Ticinese/San Lorenzo, in the Zona Tortona and along the Navigli and Via Vigevano. Other popular meeting places are a number of bars, often small and full, some also with a small kitchen, where dedicated bartenders mix excellent cocktails. There are several good addresses for live music, and in summer the parks also come to life with music and events.

BARS & WINE BARS

BICERÌN (134 C4) (*ⁿ⁰ L3*)

At around 5pm in the lively quarter north-east of the Giardini Pubblici the "Coffee and chocolate drink" opens its doors. Visitors come to the lounge bar for a glass of good wine or the latest ✪ Oscar.697 organic vermouth with fresh mint or elderflower. Food is also available. *Daily | Via Panfilo Castaldi 24 | tel. 02 84 25 84 10 | www.bicerinmilano.com | Metro 1 Porta Venezia | Metro 3 Piazza Repubblica*

INSIDER TIP BLENDERINO
(133 F3) (*Ⓜ K2*)

Tiny, very pretty bar with first-class aperitifs and cocktails until late at night; a highlight in the somewhat touristy corner near the Corso Como. *Closed Mon | Piazza XXV Aprile 14 | Metro 2 Moscova*

CANTINE ISOLA (133 D3) (*Ⓜ H2*)

Small wine store with bar in the middle of the Chinese quarters. It's where the young Milanese learn to drink wine – an

restaurant. *Daily | Viale Ceresio 7 | tel. 02 31 03 92 21 | www.ceresio7.com | Metro 2 Porta Garibaldi, Moscova | tram 2, 4*

IL GATTOPARDO CAFÉ (132 C2) (*Ⓜ G2*)

On the altar of the DJ's console: it's unlikely that this church ever imagined it would one day be a glamorous location for aperitifs and dancing. Book for aperitifs (tel. 02 34 53 76 99)! *Closed Mon | Via Piero della Francesca 47 | www.ilgattopardocafe.it | bus 33, 43, 57*

The lounge bar Living on the Parco Sempione, attracts a constant stream of thirsty people

institution. *Closed Mon | Via Paolo Sarpi 30 | Metro 5 Monumentale | bus 94 | tram 2, 12*

CERESIO 7 ★ (133 E2) (*Ⓜ J2*)

Up here, on the roof of the former electricity authority, you'll feel you've arrived in the glamorous, ultra-cool Milan: with a drink in your hand, some tartar and sushi delights at one of the two pools under the starry sky, views of the illuminated Monumental Cemetery and the glowing high-rise towers at the Porta Nuova. The lounge bar also has a chic

H-CLUB DIANA (135 D4) (*Ⓜ M3*)

Retro chic and funky: a popular address for aperitifs at this fabulous old Liberty-style hotel. The large windows open up in summer, and *la bella gente* takes its cocktails into the lovely garden. *Closed Sun | Viale Piave 42 | tel. 0 22 05 80 81 | www.hclub-diana.it | Metro 1 Porta Venezia | tram 9*

LIVING ● (133 D4) (*Ⓜ H3*)

Elegant yet comfortable lounge bar where you can also dine. In summer, you can also sit outside and enjoy the views of the Arco della Pace in Sempione Park. Be sure to book for Happy Hour and the generous buffet (tel. 02 33 10 08 24)!! *Closed Mon | Piazza Sempione 2 | www.livingmilano.com | bus 1, 57, 61*

MAG CAFÈ (137 D5) *(⨔ H7)*

First-class original drinks, good music, and snacks for when you're feeling peckish: the highly recommended cocktail bar, one of the many pubs, bars and restaurants on the banks of the Naviglio. And if you'd like to sip your cocktails with just your loved one, you can book the tiniest bar in Milan right next door. *Daily | Ripa di Porta Ticinese 43 | Metro 2 Porta Genova*

INSIDER TIP MOM CAFÈ
(139 D3) *(⨔ M6)*

A tip from the locals: for years, this large bar has been buzzing at cocktail hour and beyond. A young spirit, open to all; a generous buffet, and bunches of happy people on the pavement. *From 6pm | Viale Monte Nero 51 | tel. 02 59 90 15 62 | Metro 3 Porta Romana | tram 9*

MORNA (136 C4) *(⨔ G7)*

This much-loved neighbourhood pub is a surprising sight in the otherwise cool designer quarter Tortona. You'll soon strike up a conversation with locals over a beer at the bar, or you can watch your neighbours playing boccia. *Closed Sun | Via Tortona 21 | Metro 2 Porta Genova*

NOTTINGHAM FOREST COCKTAIL BAR ★ (135 D6) *(⨔ M4)*

If you like ranking lists: this tiny, dimly lit cult bar is said to be one of the 50 best cocktail bars in the world. Every single drink is presented as a miniature theatrical piece: perhaps in a trainer, perhaps squeezed out of a toothpaste tube – or

sipped from a tiny bathtub. *Closed Mon | Viale Piave 1 | www.nottingham-forest. com | Metro 1 Palestro | tram 9*

RITA & COCKTAILS ★ (136 C5) *(⨔ H7)*

This pub down a side street of the Navigli uses selected ingredients to mix exceptional drinks. Also good music and plenty of regulars – an extremely popular cocktail bar. *Daily | Via Angelo Fumagalli 1 | Metro 2 Porta Genova*

DISCOTHEQUES & CLUBS

Clubs normally open at 8pm and discotheques from 10pm or 11pm, entrance from 15 euros (includes a drink).

★ **Nottingham Forest Cocktail Bar**
Consider yourself really lucky if you get a table at this trendy mini-sized bar → p. 73

★ **Ceresio 7**
Milan's coolest cocktail location in summer → p. 72

★ **Teatro alla Scala**
Milan's opera house: the experience of a lifetime → p. 75

★ **Rita & Cocktails**
Good cocktails and a great atmosphere at the Navigli → p. 73

★ **Piccolo Teatro**
The most important theatre in Italy → p. 75

★ **Blue Note**
Live jazz every evening – an institution → p. 75

MARCO POLO HIGHLIGHTS

BOBINO CLUB (136 B5) *(Ⓜ F7)*
Next to the Naviglio: people come for Happy Hour and to eat – and stay to dance on hip-hop, electro and revival evenings. The mood is even better at the garden parties in summer. *Thu–Sun | Alzaia Naviglio Grande 116 | Metro 2 Porta Genova | bus 74, 325 | tram 2*

BYBLOS (133 D2) *(Ⓜ H1)*
One of the chic, expensive discos with VIP and model appearances. Lounge area, restaurant and summer terrace. *Closed Mon–Wed | Via Messina 38 | www.byblosmilano.com | tram 12, 14*

JUST CAVALLI CLUB (133 D5) *(Ⓜ H3)*
This glamorous dinner and disco club, the brainchild of fashion designer Rober- to Cavalli, is situated at the foot of the Torre Branca lookout tower in Parco Sempione. Guests sit on antelope fur and dance under bright steel and light installations; dancing outside as well in summer. *Daily | Via Luigi Camoens | milano.cavalliclub.com | Metro 1, 2 Cadorna | bus 61*

VOLT (133 F3) *(Ⓜ J2)*
When it comes to clubbing. Milan is currently streets ahead of everyone else. The "in" clubs are Dude and Wall. This one here in Brera has the very best DJ gigs. For the programme, go to Facebook and volt.club.milano. *Via Alessandro Volta 9 | Metro 2 Moscova*

CINEMA

All the premiere cinemas are in the city centre while the large cinema complexes are situated on the outskirts. Tickets cost between 5 and 12 euros. The *Cinema Anteo* (133 F3) *(Ⓜ K2)* *(Via Milazzo 9 | www.spaziocinema.info | Metro 2 Moscova)* is a meeting place for Milanese film buffs with its undubbed versions, its own *osteria* (megascreen for TV coverage) and bookstore.

CONCERTS & OPERA

In addition to classical concert halls such as the *Auditorium di Milano* you can also experience concerts and choirs in churches such as the *Chiesa Protestante, Santa Maria della Passione, San Marco* or INSIDER TIP *San Maurizio al Monastero Maggiore* (fantastic atmosphere!) *(www.lacappellamusicale.com)*. The Conservatorio is the venue for chamber music concerts by Quartetto di Milano *(www.quartettomilano.it)*. Currently the most highly regarded symphony orchestra, the Orchestra Verdi *(www.laverdi.org)*, usually plays at the *Auditorium di Milano* (137 E6) *(𝄞 J8) (16–42 euros, more for special concerts | Largo Gustav Mahler | tram 3, 9 | bus 59, 71)*. Im modernen *Teatro degli Arcimboldi* (0) *(𝄞 0) (Viale dell'Innovazione 20 | teatroarcimboldi.it | S 9 Greco Pirelli)* in the former industrial area of Bicocca, you can enjoy mainstream theatre productions and variety shows.

TEATRO ALLA SCALA ★
(131 D2–3) *(𝄞 K4)*

The neo-classical opera house has been completely renovated and extended by the architect Mario Botta. Tickets (from 20–250 euros) can be booked online *(www.teatroallascala.org)*, while the booking office *(daily noon–6pm | in the basement of the Duomo Metro station | Galleria del Sagrato)* sells last-minute tickets. The box office *(Via Filodrammatici 2 | tel. 02 72 00 37 44)* opens 2.5 hours before show time.

LIVE MUSIC & JAZZ

Entrance fee depends on the event (most start at 9.30pm or 10pm) from 10 euros.

ALCATRAZ (133 E1) *(𝄞 J1)*
It has a capacity of several thousand, all here for the live concerts – and they don't want to be disappointed. Three days a week, on Tue, Wed and Thu, the potent sound system plays international underground groups. *Disco on Fri and Sat. Via Valtellina 21 | www.alcatrazmilano.com | tram 3*

BLUE NOTE ★ (133 F1) *(𝄞 K1)*
National and international jazz greats perform in this jazz club with restaurant in the Isola district, the Sunday brunch with live music is also very popular *(reservations recommended! tel. 02 69 01 68 88). Daily | Via Pietro Borsieri 37 | www.blue*

notemilano.com | Metro 2, 3 Porta Garibaldi, Zara

CIRCOLO MAGNOLIA (0) *(𝄞 0)*
Live concerts are stage in the middle of May under the starry sky in the large city park Idroscalo in the suburb of Segrate. There's a festival mood on every evening, and prices are low. Food and drinks are available until daybreak. *Via Circonvallazione Idroscalo 41 | www.circolomagnolia.it | LIN night train from Porta Venezia to Parco Idroscalo | bus 73*

INSIDER TIP ▶ NIDABA THEATRE
(137 D5) *(𝄞 H7)*

Tiny music club that is always full, live performances every evening (blues, soul, rockabilly, jazz, country, folk). Excellent beer and atmosphere. *Closed Sun/Mon | Via Emilio Gola 12 | www.nidaba.it | tram 3*

THEATRE

Look out for performances at the Teatro dell'Elfo Puccini *(www.elfo.org)* and at the interesting cultural centre Teatro Franco Parenti *(www.teatrofrancoparenti.it)*. Experimental performances are staged at the *Teatro dell'Arte (at the Triennale Design Museum | www.triennale.org/teatro)*. For classical ballet with its own dance company, go to the *Teatro di Milano (www.teatrodimilano.it)*.

PICCOLO TEATRO ★
The leading theatre in Italy was founded by Paolo Grassie and Giorgio Strehler in 1947. Now, there are also jazz concerts. Plays are held in three venues: (130 C3) *(𝄞 J4) Via Rovello 2 | Metro 1 Cairoli;* (130 C1) *(𝄞 J3) Via Rivoli 6 | Metro 2 Lanza;* (130 B1) *(𝄞 J3) Largo Antonio Greppi 1 | Metro 2 Lanza | alle tel. 02 42 41 18 89 | www.piccoloteatro.org | tickets 22–40 euros*

WHERE TO STAY

Of course Milan has a whole range of wonderful luxury hotels: tasteful and exquisite or ultra modern, with everything you could possibly wish for. But even if you don't stay in one of them you can still enjoy the luxury life by visiting one of the many exclusive hotels during their aperitif happy hour. Non-guests can also take advantage of their amazing spa and wellness facilities.

As business, fashion and trade fairs cause prices in Milan to rocket, the secret is to choose your dates carefully and book through one of the Internet portals. A good medium-class hotel that will set you back at least 300 euros at trade fair time may well only cost 100 euros on quiet days or at a week-end. The price differences in this city really are amazing.

Other options are apartment hotels and the many B&B offers (e.g. through *www.bed-and-breakfast.it/en/milan* or *www.bbitalia.it* and *www.airbnb.it*); prices start at 60 euros for a double room with breakfast. There are also a few cool, pleasant hostels where people also meet up to eat and listen to music. A City Tax is charged for every night's accommodation which, depending on the category, will cost another 2 to 5 euros per person. WiFi access is available in almost all of the hotels, and is usually free. Parking in the centre is very difficult, and you're unlikely to find anything for less than 25 euros a day.

Charming boutique accommodation, cool design hotels and casual hostels: living the good life on a city trip

HOTELS: EXPENSIVE

ANTICA LOCANDA DEI MERCANTI ★
(130 C3) (*J4*)

It's a 5-minute walk to the castle, and 3 minutes to Brera. The large windows of this elegant old building allow plenty of light into the generously proportioned, tastefully furnished rooms and suites. Many of them even have their own private terraces, where you can enjoy your breakfast amongst fragrant jasmine and flowering roses. An enchanting haven in the middle of the city. *15 rooms | Via San Tomaso 6 | tel. 0 28 05 40 80 | www. locanda.it | Metro 1 Cordusio*

BULGARI ★ (131 D2) (*K4*)

Pure luxury in the luxury quarter Quadrilatero, as you would expect from this jewellery brand, and a delight for the senses: the wonderful materials in natural hues are irresistible, and more than anything you want to touch the African marble and the precious woods from all over the world. Take a seat in the open-air lounge

Something for design-loving purists: a suite at the Hotel Straf

and enjoy a cocktail in the enchanting garden. Watch the pool water from one of the loveliest hammams in the city sparkle on the gold shimmering mosaics. *58 rooms. | Via Fratelli Gabba 7b | tel. 0 28 05 80 51 | www.bulgarihotels.com | Metro 3 Monte Napoleone | from 550 euros*

STARHOTEL E.C.HO. ◍
(134 C2) (*M1*)
Comfortable, modern hotel with good service at the main station, equally popular with business and leisure travellers. The fresh organic food in the restaurant balances perfectly with the energy-reducing measures and eco-friendly materials. Good Internet prices! *143 rooms. | Via Andrea Doria 4 | tel. 0 26 78 91 | www.star hotels.com | Metro 2, 3 Centrale*

ENTERPRISE (132 B1–2) (*F1*)
An extremely successful city hotel: plenty of chic design yet cosy and comfortable, top class and yet extremely affordable weekend prices. Topped only by the superb ❄ spa area with panoramic views, the aperitif hour and the excellent restaurant. You'll really feel you're in Milan. *123 rooms. | Corso Sempione 91 | tel. 02 31 81 81 | www.enterprisehotel.com | tram 1 | bus 14*

MILANO SCALA ◍ (130 C2) (*J–K4*)
Music and production designs in the stylishly elegant suites set the mood for an evening at La Scala. On the ❄ roof terrace there is an aperitif to go with the overture, and a cocktail for the finale. Despite all the comforts, the hotel places much value on energy-saving technology. *62 rooms | Via dell'Orso 7 | tel. 02 87 09 61 | www.hotelmilanoscala.it | Metro 1, 3 Cairoli, Montenapoleone*

PRINCIPE DI SAVOIA ★
(134 B3) (*L2*)
The Queen, Madonna and George Clooney have all stayed at this regal Grand Hotel in the past. The impressive classical building sits on a small hill overlooking

the inner city ring road. Everything is elegant and comfortable, with guests' every wish catered for and pampering in the perfectly equipped spa. *301 rooms. | Piazza della Repubblica 17 | tel. 0 26 23 01 | www.dorchestercollection.com | Metro 3 Repubblica*

STRAF HOTEL & BAR (131 D3) (*M K5*)
Minimalist design with bare concrete walls and plain furniture – for fans of hip purism. The sixth-floor suites have their own private mini spas. Also a INSIDER TIP popular meeting place for aperitifs with a DJ set – and only 50 m/164 ft from the cathedral square. *64 rooms | Via San Raffaele 3 | tel. 02 80 50 81 | www.straf.it | Metro 1, 3 Duomo*

HOTELS: MODERATE

MAISON BORELLA (137 D4) (*M H7*)
At this tasteful boutique hotel with a decidedly French flair, you'll be close to the Naviglio and in the midst of the picturesque Milanese entertainment district. At the upper end of the price category. On the ground floor is the Turbigo restaurant, which is highly recommended. *24 rooms | Alzaia Naviglio Grande 8 | tel. 02 58 10 91 14 | www. hotelmaisonborella. com | Metro 2 Porta Genova*

BRERA APARTMENTS
30 apartments in the centre, most of them in Brera and around the Corso Garibaldi, spacious, well-furnished and full of urban chic. *tel. 02 36 55 62 84 | www.brerapartments.com*

ANTICA LOCANDA LEONARDO
(132 C6) (*M H5*)
This pretty boutique hotel, comfortably elegant and with a small garden, is only a few steps from Leonardo's "Last Supper". *16 rooms. | Corso Magenta 78 |* *tel. 02 48 01 41 97 | www.anticalocanda leonardo.com | Metro 1 Conciliazione | tram 16, 20 | bus 60*

UNA HOTEL MEDITERRANEO
(139 D4) (*M M7*)
The Una chain also runs a highly-recommended, pleasantly contemporary (especially on the inside) establishment in the lively city centre quarter of Porta Romana. *93 rooms. | Via Lodovico Muratori 14 | tel. 02 55 00 71 | www.unahotels.it | Metro 3 Porta Romana*

HOTEL NAPOLEON (135 E3) (*M N2*)
The location down a quiet, elegant side street off the bustling Corso Buenos Aires shopping area is ideal, as is the particularly charming stroll from here to the city centre. Everything inside the pretty, old building is fresh and very stylish. A pleasant hotel for a city trip. Excellent value for money. *40 rooms. | Via Federico Ozanam 12 | tel. 02 29 52 03 66 | www. hotelnapoleonmilano.com | Metro 1 Lima*

⭐ **Ostello Bello**
City-centre meeting place for backpackers and music-lovers
→ **p. 82**

⭐ **Principe di Savoia**
Ironically, this regal luxury hotel just happens to be on the Piazza della Repubblica → **p. 78**

⭐ **Bulgari**
The gem: pure luxury with the most precious materials → **p. 77**

⭐ **Antica Locanda dei Mercanti**
Small establishment that is bursting with atmosphere
→ **p. 77**

MARCO POLO HIGHLIGHTS

B&B DI PORTA TOSA (0) (*⑳ O5*)
Rather than being in the heart of the city, like most Milanese you'll be in a residential area with bus and tram stops outside the front door. Everything in this carefully renovated old apartment has been carefully chosen with exquisite taste – the fabrics, the vintage furniture. And you'll be pampered with a first-class breakfast. At the bottom end of the price category. *4 rooms. | Via Annibale Grasselli 11 | tel. 34 76 49 35 72 | www. portatosa.it | S-Bahn Porta Vittoria | bus 45 | tram 27*

MORE THAN A GOOD NIGHT'S SLEEP

Opulence in the spirit of Verdi

Following the triumphant premières of his operas at La Scala, delighted audiences accompanied Giuseppe Verdi (1813–1901) back to the *Grand Hotel et de Milan* **(131 E3)** (*⑳ K4*) (*95 rooms | Via Alessandro Manzoni 29 | tel. 02 72 31 41 | www.grandhoteletdemilan.it | Metro 3 Monte Napoleone | Expensive*). This is where Italy's most famous opera composer headed at the end of the working day. As soon as you cross the threshold, you'll feel as if you were stepping back in time. Just imagine who else must have sat and slept in the beautiful period furniture, some of which is Art Deco, some Art Nouveau. The amazingly attentive staff also seem to be from a different era. Comfort and technology are absolutely up-to-date.

On a crooked chair

Luscious colours and design flow: star architect Matteo Thun has turned the former industrial complex in the creative district of Tortona into a contemporary city establishment. As soon as you walk into the *Nhow Hotel* **(136 C4)** (*⑳ F7*) (*249 rooms | Via Tortona 35 | tel. 0 24 89 88 61 | www.nh-hotels.it | Metro 2 Porta Genova | Moderate–Expensive*) you'll feel as if you were in a showroom for designer furniture. The young and discerning city trip clientèle appreciates this, and likewise the spaciousness of the rooms and the extensive breakfast buffet.

Normal & nice

For once, somewhere that isn't an ultra-cool designer spot, but a cheerfully run family hotel with well-kept, comfortable rooms: *Sanpi* **(134 C4)** (*⑳ M3*) (*79 rooms | Via Lazzaro Palazzi 18 | tel. 02 29 51 33 41 | www.hotelsanpimilano.it | Metro 1 Porta Venezia | Moderate*). English is spoken at reception; breakfast is Italian, and you can relax after the day's endeavours in the small green courtyard. Head to the nearby Giardini Pubblici for a jog in the morning.

A healthy sleep

You'll sleep well here and with a clear conscience. Every single detail at pretty little ⊛ *Bio City Hotel* **(0)** (*⑳ O*) (*17 rooms | Via Edolo 18 | tel. 02 66 70 35 95 | www.biocityhotel.it | Metro 3 Sondrio | bus 43 | Budget–Moderate*) in a residential quarter behind the main railway station matches its eco concept, such as building and furniture materials, the fabrics, the paints, the energy supply and the cleaning products. And, of course, the excellent fresh breakfast. Allergy-sufferers can also breathe easy here.

WHERE TO STAY

ANTICA LOCANDA SOLFERINO
(133 F3–4) (*K3*)
Small, old-fashioned hotel that is very popular with regularly, full of atmosphere in the former artists' quarter of Breda; often fully booked well in advance. *11 rooms | Via Castelfidardo 2 | tel. 02 65 70 129 | www.anticalocandasolferino.it | Metro 2,3 Moscova*

UNA HOTEL TOCQ
(133 F2–3) (*J –K2*)
Smaller establishment of the new Una chain close to the entertainment and shopping street Corso Como and the new high-rise enclave of Porta Nuova. Great fluctuations between trade fair and normal prices. *122 rooms | Via Alessio di Tocqueville 7 d | tel. 02 62 071 | www.una hotels.it | Metro 2 Porta Garibaldi*

HOTELS: BUDGET

ACCA PALACE (0) (*0*)
Quietly located in the north-west with an underground station nearby. Good for travellers with a car, as it has its own car park. Fresh, spacious rooms (with a kitchenette); excellent value for money. *44 rooms | Via Giovanni Nicotera 9 | tel. 02 64 66 62 39 | www.accapalace.com | Metro 3 Affori Centro*

CESENA 5 (0) (*G1*)
With its six stylish rooms, this is more a small hotel than a B&B. Friendly owner, quiet location in the north-west Ghisolfa area, with good public transport links. *Via Cesena 5 | tel. 3 35 38 84 17 | www. cesena5.com | Metro 2 Lanza tram | 12*

B&B COCOON
(136 C4) (*G6*)
Three beautiful rooms in the trendy Tortona district close to the Navigli – ideal for a romantic city visit for two. *Via*

Ageless and exquisite: Verdi's favourite hotel Grand Hotel et de Milan

Voghera 7 | tel. 02 83 22 769 | www. cocoonbb.com | Metro 2 Porta Genova

DELIZIA (139 F1) (*O5*)
A simply, pleasant, well-priced little hotel in a quiet, neat residential area not far from the centre – what more could you want? *14 rooms. | Via Archimede 86–88 | tel. 02 74 05 44 | www.hoteldelizia.com | bus 54, 92*

ESCO (134 C2) *(📖 M2)*

Some of the rooms in this little multi-floor hostel overlook the vast railway station. The friendly young managers and cheerful design contribute to its modern freshness. *10 rooms. | Via Antonio da Recanate 2 | tel. 02 83 43 96 30 | www.hotelesco.it | Metro 2, 3 Stazione Centrale | bus 60 | tram 5, 9*

GIOIA HOUSE (135 D4) *(📖 M3)*

Close to the Corso Buenos Aires shopping street is this particularly appealing guesthouse with large and small rooms, three of which share a bathroom. Breakfast includes delicious cakes baked by the landlady. *6 rooms. | Via Lazzaro Spallanzani 6 | tel. 02 83 42 01 50 | www.gioiahouse.com | Metro 1 Porta Venezia*

MILANO NAVIGLI (137 E4) *(📖 J7)*

Although it is situated above McDonald's, it is none the less an appealing, modern city hotel in a fabulous location close to the Porta Ticinese with views of the Piazza XXIV Maggio and Darsena, the Navigli harbour. At the upper end of the price category. *22 rooms. | Piazza Sant' Eustorgio 2 | tel. 02 36 55 37 51 | www.hotelmilano navigli.it | tram 3, 9*

OSTELLO BELLO ★ (130 B5) *(📖 J5)*

This hostel really does deserve its name of "lovely hostel": situated down a side street off Via Torino; a relaxed, comfortable atmosphere, delicious food, free WiFi and live concerts on Tuesday and Wednesday evenings. *10 rooms. | Via Medici 4 | tel. 02 36 58 27 20 | www.ostel lobello.com | tram 2, 3*

LA RESIDENZA ⊕ (0) *(📖 0)*

In the north of Milan, this hotel belongs to the EcoWorldHotel group – they even have a suite done out according to feng shui principles and they also serve breakfasts made from organic produce. *60 rooms | Via Vittorio Scialoia 3 | tel. 02 64 16 46 | www.residenzahotel.it | Metro 3 Affori Centro*

SAN FRANCISCO (135 F2) *(📖 O1)*

Much about this establishment is good at its favourable price: close to the university, friendly atmosphere, fresh, well-kept rooms.

VIETNAMONAMOUR (135 F3) *(📖 O2)*

A Vietnamese lady and a man from Milan have created this enchanting oasis in a quiet residential area. **Four B&B**

LOW BUDGET

There is a branch of the *Ostello Bello* near the station with 198 beds in rooms for 2 to 6 occupants called the *Ostello Bello Grande* **(134 C2)** *(📖 M2)* *(from 38 euros | Via Roberto Lepetit 33 | tel. 02 67 05 92 1 | www.ostello bello.com | Metro 2, 3 Stazione Centrale)*. Despite being spread over six floors, it's lovely, relaxed and clean.

Formerly a military barracks, now the industrial-style INSIDER**TIP** *Madama Hostel* **(139 D6)** *(📖 N8)* *(60 beds in rooms of 2 to 6 | Via Benaco 1 | tel. 02 36 72 73 70 | www.madamahostel. com | Metro 3 Lodi Tibb | bus 65)*: a cool meeting place with a bistro and music club near the Fondazione Prada art foundation.

For more low-cost accommodation, go to the web portal *it.hostelbookers. com/ostelli/italia/milano*.

Deluxe wellness oasis: the spa at the Bulgari Hotel is also open to non-residents

rooms and a Vietnamese restaurant in the garden. The wooden furniture with marquetry and the silk fabrics were all hand-made in Vietnam. *Via Alessandro Pestalozza 7 | tel. 02 70 63 46 14 | www. vietnamonamour.com | Metro 2 Piola*

TIME TO CHILL

Want to be pampered with style? You can at the luxury hotels whose wonderful spas are also open to non-residents: such as the Bulgari (see p. 77). There are fabulous views from the ✂ *Spa Terme di Kyoto* of the hotel *Enterprise* (see p. 78). The spa at the Boscolo Milano **(131 E3)** *(Ⓜ K4) (Corso Giacomo Matteotti 4–6 | tel. 02 77 67 96 10 | milano.boscolohotels.com | Metro 1 San Babila)* is decidedly futuristic. Beauty treatments, massages, thermal baths, a sauna in a vintage tram and a garden against the old city wall by the Porta Romana, plus a daily aperitif with a fresh buffet, and a breakfast buffet for early-risers on Sundays: all this is available at the ● *QC Terme Milano* **(138 C4)** *(Ⓜ L7) (daily 9.30am–midnight | Piazzale Medaglie d'Oro 2 | www.termemilano.com | Metro 3 Porta Romana)*. A lifestyle manager (from 50 euros) provides access to the ✂ *Armani Spa* **(131 E2)** *(Ⓜ K4) (Via Alessandro Manzoni 31 | tel. 02 88 83 88 60 | Metro 3 Monte Napoleone)* in elegant shades of brown, graphite, black and sand. 1000 m/3281 ft overlooking the city; pool, sauna, steam bath and ultramodern gym.

DISCOVERY TOURS

① MILAN AT A GLANCE

START: ① Galleria Vittorio Emanuele II
END: ⑭ Navigli

Distance:
➡ almost 10 km/6 mi

1 day
walking time
(without stops)
2 ½–3 hours

COSTS: admission fees 45 euros, Metro ticket 1.50 euros

IMPORTANT TIPS: As the visit of the "Last Supper" is only permitted upon prior registration, you should plan the day according to your appointment. Here, the visit is planned for the morning.
Most museums are closed on Monday.

On this extensive tour of the centre, you'll see the loveliest parts of Milan in an exciting day. Distances in the centre are short, and you can basically walk every-where. But if needs be, it's never far to the next bus stop or taxi rank.

Would you like to explore the places that are unique to this city? Then the Discovery Tours are just the thing for you – they include terrific tips for stops worth making, breathtaking places to visit, selected restaurants and fun activities. It's even easier with the Touring App: download the tour with map and route to your smartphone using the QR Code on pages 2/3 or from the website address in the footer below – and you'll never get lost again even when you're offline.

TOURING APP

→ p. 2/3

09:00am Under the entrance to the fabulous shopping passage ❶ **Galleria Vittorio Emanuele II** → p. 35, you can enjoy a cappuccino and an aromatic *cornetto* in the legendary **Camparino in Galleria** → p. 52, the vast cathedral square in your sight.

❶ Galleria Vittorio Emanuele II

09:45am Stroll through the Galleria and on to the Piazza della Scala with the world-famous ❷ **Opera House** → p. 36, 75. This is also where you will find the magnificent town hall Palazzo Marino and the art collections

❷ Opera House

❸ Piazza Mercanti

❹ "Last Supper"

❺ Vigna di Leonardo

❻ Basilica di Sant'Ambrogio

❼ Piazzale Cadorna

❽ Castello Sforzesco

❾ Parco Sempione

of the Gallerie d'Italia, although it's better to leave them for another day. **Just before the opera house, turn left onto Via Santa Margherita,** which will take you to the atmospheric medieval ❸ **Piazza Mercanti** → p. 36. **From Piazza Cordusio, head a short way up the Via Dante, then turn left onto Via Meravigli, which extends to become the Corso Magenta.** It's about 1 km/0.6 mi to the ❹ **"Last Supper"** → p. 42 in the refectory of the impressive church of **Santa Maria delle Grazie,** past stately palazzi and the traditional **Pasticceria Marchesi** → p. 42, perhaps a good spot for a late breakfast? For prints of the "Last Supper", there's only one place to go, the stationer's INSIDER TIP **Ruffini 50 m/164 ft left of the entrance to the church.** A special discovery **on the opposite side of the Corso Magenta** is the ❺ INSIDER TIP **Vigna di Leonardo**: Leonardo da Vinci is said to have owned a wine garden here, in the enchanting garden of the equally enchanting **Casa degli Antellani** *(daily 9am–6pm | 10 euros | Corso Magenta 65).*

12:30pm **After the viewing, cross over the Via Bernardino Zenale and Via San Vittore and pass the Museum of Science** to Milan's sacral heart, the ancient ❻ **Basilica di Sant'Ambrogio** → p. 44, which you can today only admire from the outside because it is closed over lunchtime. The university is just around the corner, and the area is accordingly lively and student-y, with lots of very pleasant snack bars for a lunchtime snack.

01:30pm **Down the Via Terraggio, then the Corso Magenta and cross the ❼ Piazzale Cadorna** with Claes Oldenburg's huge pop art sculpture – a needle and thread – and in a quarter of an hour you'll come to the massive ❽ **Castello Sforzesco** → p. 38. If you want to give your feet a bit of a rest, instead take the no. 50 bus at the corner of Viale Carducci/Piazza Sant'Ambrogio for four stops, and get off at the Piazza Cairoli outside the castle. Behind the castle is the lovely ❾ **Parco Sempione** → p. 39, perfect for a stroll but also with a few sights: **if you keep to the south-west,** you'll come to the **Triennale Design Museum** → p. 41, a must in this city of design – even at this café, which is ideal for your next break, you'll sit on designer chairs. For the best views of the city, take the lift up the lookout tower **Torre Branca** → p. 41 next to the museum.

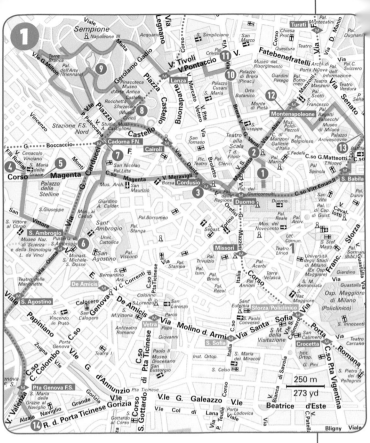

04:15pm **Exit the park on the eastern side of the castle** and you'll come to Brera. Once the artists' quarter with the major art collection ⑩ **Pinacoteca di Brera** → p. 40 and the Academy of Art, today it is one of the pleasantest quarters in the city with residential streets full of flair, with cafés, shops and art galleries. The photos in the traditional bar ⑪ **Jamaica** (Via Brera 32) bring to mind the bohemian world of bygone days.

06:15pm Early evening is dedicated to the famous fashion quarter ⑫ **Quadrilatero della Moda** → p. 60. **It's just a few steps along the Via Brera, Via Verdi and Via Manzoni**. After strolling down the Via Monte Napoleone and

⑩ Pinacoteca di Brera

⑪ Jamaica

⑫ Quadrilatero della Moda

| Bar Martini | |

| METRO 1 TO CARDONA, THEN METRO 2 TO PORTA GENOVA |

| ⑭ Navigli | |

Via della Spiga, it's time for an aperitif – the highlight in the day's routine. A glamorous venue is ⑬ **Bar Martini** in the Dolce & Gabbana flagship store at Corso Venezia 15. Then visit the various establishments, picturesquely located along the canals called the ⑭ **Navigli** → p. 45. **You can get there by subway.**

② HISTORY OF THE CITY, CULINARY DELIGHTS AND A MARBLE "MIDDLE FINGER"

START: ❶ Piazza del Duomo END: ⑪ Santa Maria della Stella	approx. 3 hours walking time (without stops) 45 minutes–1 hour
Distance: ➡ almost 3 km/2 mi	
COSTS: The museum is free of charge, but a donation is requested	

IMPORTANT TIPS: Most shops and supermarkets are closed on Sunday and ❷ San Satiro does not open before afternoon, the **museum** is open Tue–Sat 10.30am–6.30pm, ❻ San Sepolcro only Mon–Fri noon–2.30pm

The stroll through the former smart area south-west of the Piazza Duomo to the end of the Corso Magenta leads to interesting witnesses of the city's history, to contemplative and spiritual places, and some of the best food addresses in the city. All this is often hidden away down side streets, and yet still only a few steps from the major sights and tourist paths.

| ❶ Piazza del Duomo |

| ❷ Santa Maria presso San Satiro | |

From the ❶ **Piazza del Duomo** turn into the busy shopping street Via Torino which cuts through the former nobility district. During World War II many of the palaces here were destroyed, and today you can still see gaps between buildings. Fortunately the bombs spared the ❷ **Santa Maria presso San Satiro** church. At the end of the 15th century a Madonna fresco was desecrated and legend has it that after this her image began to bleed. Duke Gian Galeazzo Sforza then ordered a church to be built to house the miraculous image. In the small interior Bramante designed the illusion of an apse, using remarkable trompe l'oeil in fresco, for the Madonna's image.

The Via Torino offers some insights into the current consumer world with its many shop windows; the pavements

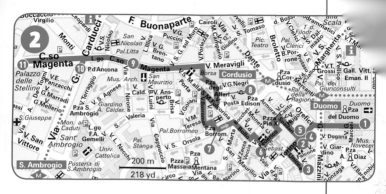

were also widened a few years back, to make it easier for people to stroll along. But other insights are also possible: **to the left, behind San Satiro, is the Via Unione (formerly Contrada dei Nobili),** whose noble past can now only be seen at no. 5 in the ❸ **Palazzo Erba Odescalchi** with its arcade-lined courtyard. Opposite, at Via Unione 6, is an old, white-tiled dairy from the 1950ers, the **Vecchia Latteria** (closed Sun and evenings | tel. 02 87 44 01 | Budget–Expensive) that serves vegetarian food; the INSIDERTIP **succulent parmigiana**, the cheese and aubergine gratin, is particularly popular.

And talking of good food: there is a veritable quarter of delicatessens down the streets north-west of the Via Torino. **Now back on the Via Torino, walk a few steps towards the cathedral square, and from the right on the Via Speronari 6** you'll catch the aromas of the crisp, freshly-baked focaccia from the ❹ **Princi** bakery, flavoured with vegetables, cheese and herbs. Wonderful delicatessens – a treat both for the eyes and for the palate – are on the other side of the Via Torino on the ❺ **Via Spadari**, elegantly flanked by Liberty-style buildings. It starts at no. 4 and the **Pescheria Spadari**, a fishmonger and eatery. Colourful macarons decorate the displays at **Ladurée** (no. 6), while **Noberasco** (no. 8) has been importing every imaginable kind of dried fruit and nut for over 100 years, and on the opposite side of the street are the windows of **Peck** → p. 64, since 1883 the delicatessen of the Milanese, which also has a restaurant and café.

Walk across the Piazza Pio XI towards the Pinacoteca Ambrosiana, at the back of which is the church of

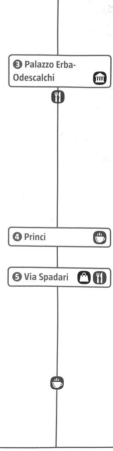

❸ Palazzo Erba-Odescalchi

❹ Princi

❺ Via Spadari

A commentary on the financial world? Maurizio Cattelan's sculpture L.O.V.E. outside the Stock Exchange

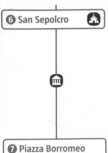

6 San Sepolcro

6 San Sepolcro. Opposite is a rather out-of-place concrete tower and balcony next to the delicate lines of a Rococo building. This is where Benito Mussolini announced the foundation of the "Fasci Italiani di Combattimento" on 23 March 1919 – the birth of the Fascist movement. Il Duce used the Fascist "speaking tower", the **Torre Litoria**, for his public appearances.

From the Piazza San Sepolcro, turn onto the Via Bollo to the junction Cinque Vie ("Five streets"). **Left along the Via Santa Maria Podone will get you to the 7 Piazza Borromeo**, once the district for the powerful noble family with the house church of **Santa Maria Podone** and opposite the converted medieval **Palazzo Borromeo**, today, still home to the family's descendants. Carlo Borromeo organised the third and last session of the Council of Trent, kept the Spanish Inquisition at bay, replacing it with his own, "milder" version, and in 1576/77 organised the care of people affected by crop failures and an outbreak of the plague, providing active and miraculous support. His cousin Federico was the founder of the Pinacoteca and the Biblioteca Ambrosiana.

From the Via Borromei (very narrow, watch out for traffic), cross the Via Santa Maria alla Porta and enjoy a

7 Piazza Borromeo

stroll around the Piazza degli Affari. Since 2010, a large marble „middle finger" has provoked outside the vast Milan Stock Exchange: the sculpture ❽ **L.O.V.E. ("Il Dito")** by the artist Maurizio Cattelan. Behind the Stock Exchange, the **Via delle Orsole takes you to the Via Meravigli, which becomes the Corso Magenta heading west.** The massive ❾ **Palazzo Litta** rises up, a noble residence in the lavish baroque and rococo form that was designed in 1648. Today it houses the headquarters of the directorate of Lombardy's cultural heritage, and the Fondazione Trussardi uses the magnificent halls for art events.

At the next junction with the Via Carducci, on the left is the Art Nouveau ❿ **Bar Magenta**, once a legendary meeting place for the Milanese. The chairs on the pavement invite passers-by to sit down and watch the goings-on. **A few steps further, already opposite Santa Maria delle Grazie, go to the former monastery complex of ⓫ Santa Maria della Stella**, the city orphanage for girls in the 17th century who were known as *stelline*, little stars. It remained an orphanage until 1971. At building no. 57, the **Museo Martinitt e Stelline** the story of how the orphans were cared for is told using old documents, photos, workshops and biographies (*martinitt* was the name for boys*)*. The most famous orphan is Leonardo del Vecchio, founder of Luxottica, the world's biggest eyewear factory. Today, the former orphanage contains a hotel, a restaurant, and stages contemporary exhibitions.

❽ L.O.V.E. ("Il Dito")

❾ Palazzo Litta

❿ Bar Magenta

⓫ Santa Maria della Stella

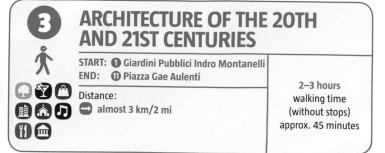

③ ARCHITECTURE OF THE 20TH AND 21ST CENTURIES

START: ❶ Giardini Pubblici Indro Montanelli
END: ⓫ Piazza Gae Aulenti

Distance:
➡ almost 3 km/2 mi

2–3 hours walking time (without stops) approx. 45 minutes

This walk includes examples of the impressive architecture of the last century, along a few very pretty city centre streets, and then on to various no less impressive buildings of the 21st century. Milan's desire for urbanistic design is particularly evident here.

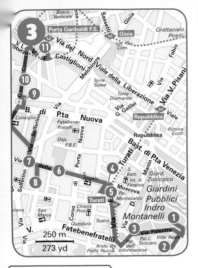

① Giardini Pubblici Indro Montanelli

② Giardini di Villa Reale

③ Centro Svizzero di Milano

④ Ca' Brutta

⑤ Palazzi Montecatini

⑥ Mediateca Santa Teresa

⑦ Palazzo del Corriere della Sera

Start on the Via Palestro at the **① Giardini Pubblici Indro Montanelli** → p. 48. This first public municipal park was designed under the Habsburg rule at the end of the 18th century, and under Napoleon the noble palace Villa Belgioioso became the Villa Reale, his residence in Milan, in 1802. It is now home to the Galleria d'Arte Moderna (GAM). Do go into the enchanting **② Giardini di Villa Reale** → p. 96, even though the park is mainly for children. The graffiti on the wall of the Padiglione d'Arte Contemporanea presents quite a contrast to this intact world: the famous street artist Blu has depicted the city as a cocaine jungle. **Continue along the Via Palestro and you'll arrive at the Piazza Cavour.** Here you will see one of the first modern high-rise buildings to be constructed after WWII, the **③ Centro Svizzero di Milano**, which has a highly-recommended bistro and lounge, the **Swiss Corner** *(daily 7.30am–2am).*

At the Piazza Cavour, take the second road on the right, the Via Turati. You'll see several impressive buildings at the point where it crosses the Via della Moscova, called **Largo Donegani or Piazza Stati Uniti:** one corner is occupied by the **④ Ca' Brutta**, the "Ugly House", a vast residential complex of 1922 that was designed by Giovanni Muzio, an important architect of the Novecento Italiano, who also designed the Triennale Design Museum. On the other side of the square, two plain and modern office blocks offer some light contrast: the **⑤ Palazzi Montecatini** by Giò Ponti, founder of the famous architecture and design magazine "Domus". One dates back to 1935–1938, the other to 1951; the latter is home to the American General Consulate.

Strolling along the lovely Via della Moscova, as you look down the streets on your right you will see the new skyline of the Porta Nuova – almost close enough to touch. Building no. 28 is home to the elegant media library **⑥ Mediateca Santa Teresa** in the Baroque church of Santa Teresa. At the junction with Via Solferino is the impressive Liberty-style **⑦ Palazzo del Corriere della Sera** of

1903, head office of the renowned Milanese daily news-paper. You could follow the journalists in their lunch breaks, e.g. **to the Via San Marco (back a turning)** to the tiny, traditional **❽ Latteria San Marco** *(closed Sat/Sun | Via San Marco 24 | tel. 0 26 59 76 53 | Moderate)* for steaming soups and pot roasts. But you won't go hungry if you're unable to find a seat there: you'll find lots of little bistros and excellent traditional establishments **on the Via Montebello or Via Solferino**, such as the modern **Pisacco** *(daily | Via Solferino 48 | tel. 02 91 76 54 72 | Budget–Moderate)*.

❽ Latteria San Marco 🍽

Refreshed and fortified, continue along the Via Marsala to the large, stage-like Piazza 25 Aprile with the Porta Garibaldi of 1828. To your right is the gastronomic world of **❾ Eataly → p. 63** and further along, at Corso Como 10, the creative world of the eponymous **❿ concept store → p. 64**. The short shopping promenade Corso Como, also a popular destination in the evenings, leads directly to the **Torre Unicredit**, with its 231m high tower Italy's tallest skyscraper. The **Porta Nuova → p. 41** high-rise group of 2012 also includes INSIDER TIP two vertically greened residential towers and the all-glass administrative building of the region of Lombardy. The connecting hinge is the **⓫ Piazza Gae Aulenti → p. 41**, named after a famous Milanese architect, where people gather in the evenings for spur-of-the-moment dance events. Under the square is a supermarket, and behind the new buildings the heart of the district Isola – an entirely different, alternative scene.

❾ Eataly 🛍
❿ 10 Corso Como 🛍 🏢
⓫ Piazza Gae Aulenti 🎵

Milan of the 21st century: high-rise ensemble Porta Nuova on the Piazza Gae Aulenti

4 ANCIENT CHURCHES AND "IN" SCENE

START: ➊ Sant'Ambrogio
END: ➊ Sant'Ambrogio

Distance:
🚶 almost 4 km/2.5 mi

2 ½ hours
walking time
(without stops)
approx. 1 hour

A short walk down side streets links the two main basilicas from the days of early Christianity, Sant'Ambrogio and San Lorenzo. They were built on the outskirts of the Roman city, partly from antique building materials, partly on antique cult sites. Ironically, this part of the city is particularly lively today, with shopping streets and precincts, unusual shops, and bars and eateries of every kind.

➊ Sant'Ambrogio

A visit to the basilica of ➊ **Sant'Ambrogio** → p. 44 is one of the most intense experiences that a visit to Milan has to offer. **You can leave the church through the side exist behind the statue of Pope Pius IX in the side aisle on the right, and a small path (buildings of the catholic university on your left) will take you to the Via Lanzone and on to the Via Caminadella:** a romantic little café in a

Lombardy Romanesque: the churchyard of the Basilica of Sant'Ambrogio

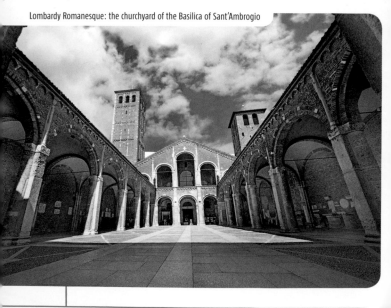

pretty courtyard serves excellent quiches at lunchtime: **❷ Caminadella Dolci** → p. 63.

Now you'll come to the lively Piazza della Resistenza Partigiana – on the corner of Corso Genova is the lovely old bar and café **❸ Cucchi** *(closed Mon)*, which serves delicious brioches filled with almond cream. **A few metres further down the Corso Genova, Via Calocero is on the right.** If you are here at aperitif time, head left down the *Via Torti 23* and pop into the relaxed **Art Bar Le Biciclette**. **Via Calocero continues to the Church of ❹ San Vincenzo in Prato**, a rebuilt Roman basilica of the 9th century that was in fact used as a chemical plant in the 19th century.

Then behind the church you can go from the Via Ariberto and the Via Marco d'Oggiono to the Corso Genova which has many interesting shops and, on the left, a covered food market. **On the right is the Via Conca del Naviglio** behind the fence you will see the small harbour basin **❺ Conca del Naviglio**, where marble for the construction of the cathedral was loaded. **The Via Scaldasole (behind the supermarket) then leads you to the Corso di Porta Ticinese and the ❻ Sant'Eustorgio** → p. 33 **Pass it on the right** and you will come to the very elegant **❼ INSIDERTIP Parco delle Basiliche** (official name Parco Papa Giovanni Paolo II). Here, people sit on benches under rose arbours with views of the back of **❽ San Lorenzo Maggiore** → p. 33, with a good view of the irregular apse chapel that has grown around the church over the centuries. Then explore the interior of the basilica.

The church piazza at the Corso Porta Ticinese is today a meeting place for youngsters and the alternative scene. Lots of pubs open in the area in the evenings. **Now walk along the ❾ Via Mora**, a street with interesting shops such as **Mimma Gini** with beautiful hand-woven fabrics, **Gardenia**, an enchanting flower shop that also serves coffee and the vintage shop **Cavalli e Nastri** → p. 68. **Continue along the Via Orazio and Via Lanzone, and you'll arrive back at ❶ Sant'Ambrogio.**

❷ Caminadella Dolci

❸ Cucchi

❹ San Vincenzo in Prato

❺ Conca del Naviglio

❻ Sant'Eustorgio

❼ Parco delle Basiliche

❽ San Lorenzo Maggiore

❾ Via Mora

❶ Sant'Ambrogio

TRAVEL WITH KIDS

With the density of its buildings, the traffic and the courtyards with attendants, Milan is not an easy city for children. However, a wide range of child-appropriate activities are organised for them; visit the tourist office for further information. There are play areas in the city parks and many of the other, smaller ones. Children under six years of age are allowed to use the city's public transport for free and adults may take up to two children in the 6–10 age group with them for free on their ticket.

INSIDER TIP GIARDINI PUBBLICI IN-DRO MONTANELLI (134 B–C4) *(ᗰ L3)*

A large city park in the city centre that is a family-friendly destination with lots of shady trees, playgrounds and large lawn areas, refreshment kiosks and fairground rides. The ● *Museo Civico di Storia Naturale (Tue–Sun 9am–5.30pm | 5 euros, children under 18 years and everyone generally free on Tue from 2pm | Corso Venezia 55)* is in the park and has 23 departments from botany to zoology and also offers a children's programme. *Daily 6.30am–8pm, in the summer until 11pm | entrances: Via Manin, Via Palestro, Corso Venezia, Bastioni di Corso Venezia | Metro 1, 3 Palestro, Porta Venezia, Turati*

GIARDINI DI VILLA REALE
(131 F1) *(ᗰ L3–4)*

A few more steps, and you will come to this romantic park around the Villa Reale where – according to the sign at the entrance – adults are only allowed in if accompanied by a child. Dogs are not allowed in at all. *Daily 9am–4pm, in the summer until 7pm | Via Palestro 15 | Metro 1 Palestro*

IDROSCALO (PARCO AZZURRO)
(140 C4) *(ᗰ 0)*

Around an artificial lake that was built in the 1920s, originally as a landing site for seaplanes, a leisure and pleasure park has been opened outside the city at Linate airport with INSIDER TIP swimming, paddling and surfing, and the water play park *Acqua Play (mid June–mid Sept)*. To the north of the park is the *Europark (in the summer daily from 8.30pm)* amusement park. *www.idroscalomilano.com | bus 73*

LEOLANDIA
(140 C3) *(ᗰ 0)*

The theme park in Capriate, which is located near the Milan-Venice motorway offers themed worlds such as pirates, cowboys, Leonardo da Vinci's

Water features, mini Italy and a park that adults may only enter if accompanied by a child

universe, rides, animals, "Minitalia" mini Italy, and much more. *Very staggered opening times, April–July usually Wed–Sun 9.30am–6pm Aug daily 10am–7pm Sept/ Oct usually Sat/Sun 10am–6pm | depending on offer, 15.50–37.50 euros, children (90–120 cm/2.9 –3.9 ft) 12.50–32.50 euros, under 90 cm/2.9 ft free | Via Vittorio Veneto 52 | www.leolandia.it*

MUSEO DEI BAMBINI ●
(138 C2–3) (*(∅ M6*)
The stage-like setting of the classic complex Rotonda della Besana contains the Children's Museum with fabulous exhibitions, animations and "play laboratories". With a small surrounding park with various arcades and a pretty café, it is an absolute treat. *Tue-Fri 9.30–18, Sat/ Son 10am–18pm | 6 euros, children 8 euros | Via Enrico Besana 12 | www.muba.it | tram 9, 12, 27 | bus 73, 77, 84*

PARCO ITTICO PARADISO
(140 C4) (*(∅ 0*)
Birds, small mammals and above all fish in a kind of underwater zoo are to be found in this animal park in Zelo Buon Persico near Paullo in south-east Milan. *March–Sept Mon–Fri 9am–5.30pm, Sat/ Sun 9am–7pm | 10 euros, children 8 euros, children up to 3 years free | Villa Pompeiana district | www.parcoittico.it*

VOLANDIA – MUSEO DEL VOLO
(140 A3) (*(∅ 0*)
The aviation museum at Malpensa airport is housed in an old aircraft factory, on display are historic aircraft models and there is also a planetarium, a flight simulator, as well as a playground and a café. *Tue–Sun 10am–7pm | 11 euros, children from 3 years and up 5 euros | Via per Tornavento 15 | Somma Lombardo | www. volandia.it*

LOMBARDY

The mountains of Lombardy even include a 4000-metre/13,000-feet peak, Pizzo Bernina (4049 m/13,284 ft), which it shares with Switzerland. Then there are charming hills, an almost subtropical lakeland, and a fertile plain with lots of rivers.

The lovely old towns of Bergamo, Cremona and Mantua are true finds. Charming squares with cafés and shops in towns like Vigevano, Lodi and Crema prove the Lombardians really know how to live. And the popular holiday destinations on the northern Italian lakes have been charming travellers since Goethe's time. With nearly 9 million citizens, Lombardy (Italian: Lombardia) is the most densely populated region in Italy and in Europe. It covers an area of 9200mi² and Milan is the regional capital. Densely populated, industrial belts, a network of often gridlocked roads, and yet: Lombardy is also surprisingly green. And wherever you go, there is something to discover: a largely unknown chapel on the Lago d'Iseo, a bathing beach on the banks of the Ticino, a historic industrial settlement or pretty trattoria, lovely beach promenades beside the major lakes, quiet, poplar-fringed paths beside the rivers Po, Adda, Ticino, Oglio or Mincio. There are cycle paths along some river banks *(www.lecicloviedelpo.movimentolento. it)*, and on Sundays on particularly attractive sections of the rivers, **INSIDER TIP** boat trips (for further information, see the various tourist offices or go to *www. navigareinlombardia.it*).

Old cities, young country: Lombardy is versatile and full of often surprising contrasts

With its medium-sized industry, Lombardy is economically superior to all 19 of the other regions of Italy. The unemployment rate is far below the national average. It is also an important agricultural region and Italy's largest food producer, encompassing the Lomellina rice fields on the border of Piemont in the west and the olive groves along Lake Garda in the east.

MARCO POLO also has a dedicated Lake Garda guide so this volume is limited to the core areas of Lombardy.

BERGAMO

(140 C3) The city (pop. 121,000) with its ★ old town, high above the centre, is truly glorious.

Nestled between the Po Valley and the foothills of the Alps – at the end of the lush Brembo and Serio valleys – Bergamo had a brief time as a free municipality before coming under Venetian rule up until 1796. The resultant blend of Lombardian and Venetian elements is what

Bergamo's main square is old – which is also what it is called: Piazza Vecchia

makes this area so unique. The familiar figure of Arlecchino from Goldoni's comedies comes from Bergamo. While the modern lower town in the plain – with lively shopping streets and the precious art gallery Accademia Carrara – has stretched out ever further, Bergamo Città Alta, the old town on the hill, has largely been preserved. The best way to get to the old city is by funicular from the Viale Vittorio Emanuele II or by walking from the parking lot at the former Sant'Agostino church.

SIGHTSEEING

ACCADEMIA CARRARA DI BELLE ARTI
For lovers of old art, a visit to this amazing art collection in the modern lower town is a must: there are works by artists including Sandro Botticelli, Giovanni Bellini, Andrea Mantegna and Titian, as well as Giovanni Battista Moroni (1522–1579) who was important in Bergamo. *Wed–Mon 10am–7pm, in winter to 5.30pm | 10 euros | Piazza Giacomo Carrara 82 | www.accademiacarrara.bergamo.it*

CAPPELLA COLLEONI
The Renaissance chapel at the cathedral square in the Città Alta was built by Giovanni Antonio Amadeo as a family burial chapel for a Venetian military leader and his daughter in 1476. The interior shows how different styles can complement each other e.g. the baroque frescoes by Gaimbattista Tiepolo (1733). *Tue–Sun 9am–12.30pm and 2pm–4.30pm, in the summer until 6.30pm*

PIAZZA VECCHIA
The chime of the Campanone calls you to the medieval ☆ tower between the Palazzo della Ragione (now the town hall) and the Palazzo del Podestà – for the views, of course! This delightful old piazza and the cathedral square form the heart of the upper town. At the centre is a Baroque fountain. The cafés and restaurants are lovely places to sit in comfort, watch the world go by and enjoy pure pleasure.

SANTA MARIA MAGGIORE
The picturesque Romanesque building (12th century) does not have a façade. In front of the portal is a beautiful porch from the 14th century. An interesting feature of the beautiful interior are the inlaid choir stalls partially designed by Lorenzo Lotto (1522–55). *Mon–Sat 9am–noon, 2.30pm–5pm, in summer until 6pm, Sun 9am–1pm and 3pm–6pm | Piazza Duomo*

FOOD & DRINK

IL CIRCOLINO DI CITTÀ ALTA
This lovely, lively restaurant is a popular meeting place that serves delicious local

cuisine – stuffed pasta, *casoncelli* or the excellent cheese from the Alps above Bergamo (and pizza as well, of course). *Daily | Vicolo Sant'Agata 19 | tel. 035 21 85 68 | www.ilcircolinocittaalta.it | Budget*

WHERE TO STAY

B&B ALBACHIARA
In an old townhouse with four lovely large rooms with own bathrooms. *Via Salvecchio 2 | tel. 035 23 17 71 | www. bbalbachiara.info | Budget–Moderate*

INFORMATION

Torre del Gombito | Via del Gombito 13 | tel. 035 24 22 26 | www.visitbergamo.it

WHERE TO GO

INSIDER TIP CRESPI D'ADDA (140 C3)
In Crespi about 15 km/9.3 mi south-west on the A 4 to Milan, close to the River Adda, an unusual settlement that dates back to the end of the 19th century in a historical blend of Styles (Unesco World Heritage Site) has been preserved: the residential settlement for labourers and other staff at a former textiles factory.

MONZA (140 C3)
This old Lombard royal city is situated on the road to Milan, a good 40 km/24.9 mi to the south-west (pop. 120,000). The famous iron crown of the Lombards that crowned all the Italian kings up to Napoleon is stored in the Gothic *cathedral*. In 1780, Giuseppe Piermarini built a summer residence for Austrian governors of Lombardy on the outskirts of Monza: *Villa Reale (www.reggiadimonza.it | Tue– Sun 10am–7pm, Fri until 10pm | 10–12 euros)*. The chambers of the last Italian kings are open to visitors, and there also

also interesting modern changing exhibitions. The *park (daily from 7am–sunset | admission free | bicycle hire)* of the royal villa is so big that it even contains a 6-km/3.7-mi long car racing track. Well – it is where the Italian Grand Prix takes place every year. Why not try a few laps – perhaps in a Ferrari 488 *(Information and prices: www.tempiodellavelocita.it, www. puresport.it/circuito-monza.asp)*. Information: *Palazzo Comunale | Piazza Carducci | tel. 039 32 32 22 | www.promonza.it*

SAN PELLEGRINO TERME AND VAL TALEGGIO (140–141 C–D2)
The busy 479 national road leads north into the Brembana valley and to the

---

MARCO POLO HIGHLIGHTS

★ **Old town of Bergamo**
Its historic Città Alta is quite charming → p. 99

★ **Cremona**
Famous as the home of violin maker Stradivari → p. 105

★ **Mantua**
The sprawling Palazzo Ducale – a city within a city → p. 107

★ **Sabbioneta**
A village transformed into an ideal Renaissance town → p. 109

★ **Certosa di Pavia**
A complex that is more like a castle than a monastery → p. 110

★ **Vigevano**
Soak up the atmosphere of its elegant and arcaded Piazza Ducale → p. 111

thermal baths of *San Pellegrino,* where the famous natural sparkling mineral water bubbles from deep underground. Grand hotels and casinos evoke the glorious time before World War I, when crowned heads of state and nobility relaxed in the health resorts and the European moneyed aristocracy gathered around gaming tables. After a long period of neglect, a new, very lovely spa centre *(qctermesanpellegrino.it)* with an exclusive hotel has been opened here.

North of San Pellegrino, the *Taleggio valley*, home to a famous cheese, forks to the west. By the time you get to *Vedeseta,* after travelling along a very winding ☙ road with beautiful views, you will understand why this valley with its lovely mountain pastures is also called 'Piccola Svizzera' – little Switzerland. You can buy and sample the Taleggio cheese at the cooperative *Sant'Antonio (Regetto district | tel. 0 34 54 74 67 | www.santantoniovaltaleggio.com)* and other places.

LOW BUDGET

You can save a lot on boat trips on Lake Como, Lake Maggiore and Lake Garda by making use of the regular local ferries *(www.navlaghi.it)* instead of the expensive excursion boats.

Just how many wonderful roses there are is made clear in the enchanting rose garden ● *Roseto Niso Fumagalli (Tue–Sun 10am–6pm)* left of the Villa Reale in Monza, a private paradise that costs nothing to visit.

BRESCIA

(141 E3) **At the foot of the Alps is Brescia, with a pop. of 195,000 the second-biggest city in Lombardy and with a decidedly attractive centre concealed behind its unstructured industrial belt.**
Each epoch has left its influence on the town's squares: the Roman world can be seen in the forum with the Capitolium temple, the Middle Ages in the Piazza Duomo/Piazza Paolo VI, the Venetian Renaissance in the Piazza della Loggia and the modern era in the Piazza della Vittoria – cool marble splendour from the Italian Fascist period.

SIGHTSEEING

PIAZZA DEL DUOMO (PIAZZA PAOLO VI)
The medieval town centre has an old town hall *(broletto)* that dates from the 12th century, a city tower *(Torre del Popolo)* and a venerable central church building *Rotonda (Duomo Vecchio)* in the strict style of the Romanesque (presumably from the example of the Church of the Holy Sepulchre of Jerusalem). The 'new' cathedral dates back to the Mannerism style, the transitional period between the Renaissance and the baroque.

PIAZZA DELLA LOGGIA
Under the Venetian rule of the 16th century, this harmonious square with its *clock tower (Torre dell'Orologio)* became the centre of the town. The most important building is the domed roofed *Loggia* (former town hall) in the beautiful Lombardian-Venetian Renaissance style modeled on the Palladiana basilica in Vicenza.

PINACOTECA TOSIO MARTINENGO
The gallery in a baroque noble palace from the 16th century contains mainly

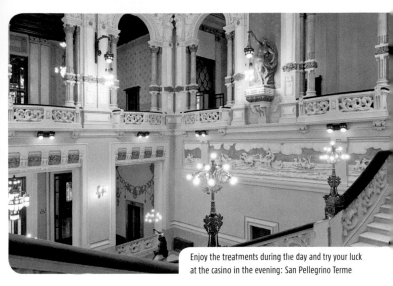

Enjoy the treatments during the day and try your luck at the casino in the evening: San Pellegrino Terme

Lombardian works, but also some Venetian paintings from the 15th–17th century, including art by Vincenzo Foppa and Lorenzo Lotto. Some of the highlights include the works by Alessandro Moretto and Girolamo Romanino of the Brescian school. Due to renovations the works are being exhibited in the Santa Giulia museum (see next entry). *Piazza Moretto 4*

INSIDER TIP SANTA GIULIA MUSEO DELLA CITTÀ

The fabulous Lombard monastery complex not only has space for two churches – San Francesco with wonderful wall murals from the 9th century and Santa Giulia from the 15th century, but for the city's museums as well. Exciting finds offer insights into the city's Celtic, Roman, Lombard, medieval history. There are also various valuable works of art. *Mid June–Sept Tue–Sun 10.30am–7pm, Oct– mid June 9.30am–5.30pm | 10 euros (12 for exhibitions) | Via dei Musei 81 b*

FOOD & DRINK

TRATTORIA AL FRATE

Traditional establishment in the centre that serves local cuisine and is open until late. Try the delicious *tortelli di zucca* (pumpkin ravioli)! Extensive wine list. closed *Mon lunchtime | Via dei Musei 25 | tel. 03 03 77 05 50 | www.alfrate.com | Budget–Moderate*

WHERE TO STAY

ALBERGO OROLOGIO 1895

This charming hotel with lovely rooms is located in an old town palazzo. *16 rooms. | Via Cesare Beccaria 17 | tel. 03 03 75 54 11 | www.albergoorologio.it | Budget*

INFORMATION

Piazza Paolo VI | Trieste 1 | tel. 03 02 40 03 57 and at the train station | www. turismobrescia.it

WHERE TO GO

CAPO DI PONTE (141 E2)

Capo di Ponte (pop. 2400) lies along the rushing river Oglio, 75 km/46.6 mi north in the Valcamonica on the SS 42. It is in the centre of an area with prehistoric petroglyphs. In the Valcamonica there are around 300,000 such rock engravings dating back to the 8th and 7th century BC. Here you will encounter the

6pm | 6 euros), the National Prehistory Museum of Valle Cominca. Capo di Ponte is about two hours from Brescia by slow train (Brescia–Iseo–Edolo line). Station: *Via Nazionale 30 | www.trenord.it*

CASTIGLIONE DELLE STIVIERE AND SOLFERINO (141 E–F4)

40 km/24.9 mi to the south-east is Solferino, and nearby is San Martino della Battaglia where the bloodiest battle of

Known more for its trendy sparkling wines than for its countryside: Franciacorta

beginning of the European human history, set against a magnificent mountain backdrop. The suburb of Naquane contains the approximately 75 acres of the *Parco Nazionale delle Incisioni Rupestri (Tue–Sun 8.30am–7pm | 4 euros),* the Naquane National Park of Rock Engravings, with around 1000 shaped rocks that can be seen on various easy routes, including the Roccia Grande with in the region of 1000 figures. At the centre is the *MUPRE (Museo Nazionale della Preistoria della Valle Camonica) (daily 2pm–*

the Italian unification took place in the summer of 1859. On the one side were the French and the Piemontese and on the other were the Austro-Hungarians. The sight of thousands of injured men inspired the Swiss philanthropist Henri Dunant, who was housed in Castiglione, to establish the Red Cross in Geneva in 1863. You can visit various museums to learn more about its history, for instance in Castiglione at the *Museo Internazionale della Croce Rossa (Tue–Sun 9am–noon and 2pm–5pm, in the summer*

3pm–6pm | 5 euros | Via Giuseppe Garibaldi 50 | www.micr.it).

INSIDER TIP **FRANCIACORTA** (141 D–F 3–4)
The champagne-like sparkling wines of the wine-growing region south of Lake Iseo are something of a cult in northern Italy. A good introduction to them is provided by the modern vinotheque with bar and restaurant *Dispensa Pani e Vini (closed Mon | Adro | Via Principe Umberto 23 | tel. 03 07 45 07 57 | www.dispensafranciacorta.com | Moderate)* in Torbiato about 30 km/18.6 mi to the north-west, or at *Erbusco*, the biggest wine store in the area that also has information on vintner visits: *Cantine di Franciacorta (www.cantinedifranciacorta.it)* on the SP XI between Rovato and Iseo.

If you have something else other than wine in mind, you can spend some time doing discount shopping in the *Franciacorta Outlet Village (daily 10am–8pm | Piazza Cascina Moie 1 | www.franciacortaoutlet.it)* in *Rodengo-Saiano*.

LAKE GARDA (LAGO DI GARDA) (141 F3)

Covering an area of 370 km²/143 mi², this is the largest lake in Italy. Protected by the Monte Baldo, the lake forms a climatic island in the foothills of the Alps, a piece of southern Italy in the north. The southern shore, with Sirmione and Desenzano, and the western shore, the most fashionable part of the lake preferred by Italians, both fall under Lombardy. Detailed information can be found in the MARCO POLO travel guide 'Lake Garda'.

LAKE ISEO (LAGO D'ISEO) (141 D3)

About 20 km/12.4 mi along the SS 510, you'll come to the eponymous lake near the little town of Iseo. In 2016, the lake, its pretty villages and hotels made headlines all over the world as the result of the art event *Floating Piers* by the packaging artist Christo. In the middle of the Lago d'Iseo is the green hill Monte Isola, Italy's biggest lake island, with lovely walks (very busy on Sundays); boat crossing from Iseo, Sulzano or Sale Marasino. In Sulzano, the hotel *Rivalago (33 rooms | Via Luigi Cadorna 7 | tel. 0 30 98 50 11 | www.rivalago.it | Moderate–Expensive)* right beside the lake is in a pretty, romantic setting. In *Pisogne* on the northern tip of the lake it is worth visiting the **INSIDER TIP** *Santa Maria della Neve* church, which is also known as the 'poor man's Sistine Chapel' because of the wonderful frescoes by Girolamo Romanino (circa 1534) that adorn its interior.

CREMONA

(141 D5) ★ **Cremona, home town (pop. 80,000) to the luthier Antonio Stradivari, its old town centre paved with river gravel and with the monumental cathedral, is one of the most popular travel destinations in Lombardy.**

The town was established during the period of the free communes, when Cremona, supported by the Emperor Barbarossa, resisted the influence of Milan. A number of string instrument workshops made the city a centre for music with a showroom on the Piazza Stradivari *(www.cremonaliuteria.it)*. You can shop for the famous *Torrone* (almond nougat) in the pedestrian zone of the Corso Matteotti with its stylish shops and then relax on one of the beautiful little ● squares, Piazza Stradivari and Piazza del Comune/Piazza del Duomo, where there are some inviting street cafés.

Cremona developed during the time of the free commune when the city, with the support of Emperor Barbarossa, was able to resist Milan's influence.

CREMONA

SIGHTSEEING

CATHEDRAL
The old Romanesque cathedral is in a delightful position in its peaceful square, and in the street café you'll feel as if you were in the middle of a medieval stage. Construction commenced in 1107 with the two-storey facade, the artistic rose window and the ornate portico. The three-aisled interior is decorated with frescoes by Lombard and Venetian masters.

Stradivari's hometown is still a centre for violin making

MUSEO CIVICO ALA PONZONE
The picture gallery with Lombard paintings from the 15th to 19th centuries is housed in the building of the Museo Civico, along with an extensive private collection of string instruments. *Tue–Son 10am–5pm | 7 euros | Via Ugolani Dati 4*

MUSEO DEL VIOLINO
On the southern edge of the old town is the modern violin museum on the history of the violin: with a valuable collection of old and new string instruments, the entire estate of Stradivari, with special exhibitions on everything to do with the violin, and with an acoustically superior concert hall, the venue for the Stradivari Festival in September. *Tue – Sun 10am–6pm | 10 euros | Piazza Guglielmo Marconi | www.museodelviolino.org*

PIAZZA DEL COMUNE
This is the heart of the town and one of the most beautiful medieval squares in Italy. The sights include the cathedral, the Gothic Torrazzo (the bell tower), the Romanesque baptistry, the Loggia dei Militi (seat of the leader of the urban militia) and the Palazzo del Comune (former seat of the municipal government). The symbol of the city and the highest bell tower 🔊 Torrazzo in Italy (111m/364ft) was built in 1267. The climb to the top is worth the effort – the views are fantastic. *Daily 10am–1pm and 2.30pm–6pm | 5 euros*

FOOD & DRINK

HOSTERIA 700
One of the reasons why the *marubini cremonesi* (ravioli) taste so delicious is because you are dining in an elegant palazzo in the middle of the town. *Mon-evening, closed Tue | Piazza Gallina 1 | tel. 037236175 | www.hosteria700.com | Moderate*

WHERE TO STAY

LOCANDA AL CARROBBIO
8 km/5 mi outside the town in fertile farmland is where you will find this comfortable country hotel that also serves excellent food. *6 rooms. | Via Castelverde 54 | tel. 03 72 56 09 63 | carrobbio.net | Budge–Moderate*

INFORMATION

Piazza del Comune 5 | tel. 03 72 40 70 81 | www.turismocremona.it

WHERE TO GO

CREMA (141 D4)

To get to Crema (pop. 35,000) you travel through the Po Valley with its landscape of poplar groves and large fields of corn and alfalfa. The town lies almost 40 km/24.9 mi to the north-west on the right bank of the Serio. It is the seat of the Catholic Bishop of Crema. From 1499–1797 it formed part of the territory of Venice, and its influence is evident in the town's buildings: the large Renaissance piazza lined with arcades and the 16th century *Palazzo del Comune* with its Venetian windows. This is also where you will find the city's main sight, the recently refurbished Lombard-Gothic *cathedral* in the region's typical brown brick. Its Renaissance bell tower still defines the town silhouette.

In the restored complex of the Augustinian monastery, there is the small town museum *Museo Civico di Crema (Tue 2pm–5.30pm, Wed–Fri 10am–noon and 2pm–5.30pm, Saat 10am–noon and 3.30pm–6.30pm, Sat/Sun 10am–noon and 3pm–6pm | admission free | Via Dante Alighieri 49)* which also often hosts important exhibitions. Also worth a visit is the pilgrimage church of *Santa Maria delle Croce*, a circular sanctuary that was built in the Bramante style in 1500, which is in the northern outskirts of town. On the Piazza Garibaldi, the *Pasticceria Treccia d'Oro (closed Wed)* sells wonderful cakes and tempting confectionaries, including the braided yeast cake, the *treccia,* a speciality of Crema. Information: *Piazza Duomo 22 | tel. 0 37 38 10 20 | www.prolococrema.it*

INSIDER TIP LODI (140 C4)

The small town (pop. 42,000) 50 km/ 31.1 mi to the north-west on the Adda, is one of undiscovered beauties of Lombardy. Worth seeing is the picturesque *Piazza della Vittoria* with the cathedral (built in 1158), the Gothic *San Francesco* church. However the highlight is in the Via Incoronata: the octagonal Renaissance church *Tempio della Beata Vergine Incoronata*, which is completely painted with biblical motifs (by artists such as by Bergognone in 1515 and the Piazza family). Bistros and restaurants are all over the centre, while the food – including fish – is excellent at the more exclusive *Ristorante La Coldana (closed Sat lunchtime and Mon | Via privata del Costino | tel. 03 71 43 17 42 | www.lucoldana.it | Moderate)* in a refurbished country house on the south-eastern edge of the city. Information: *Piazza Broletto 4 | tel. 03 71 40 92 38 | www.turismo.provincia.lodi.it*

MANTUA (MANTOVA)

(141 F5) The Mincio River lies around half the old town like a lake, a lovely sight even in the middle of misty winter. The greatest treasure of the pleasant Renaissance city of ★ Mantua (pop. 49,000) is a small painted room in the vast castle in the centre.

Under the reign of the Gonzaga royal family, in the 15th/16th century, the city became one of the most magnificent seats in Europe. The greatest artists of the time – Andrea Mantegna, Leon Battista Alberti, Giulio Romano – were employed here by the Gonzagas. Great churches like Sant' Andrea (the façade is in the form of a triumphal arch, from around 1470) and San Sebastiano (begun in 1460, in a strictly classical style) were commissioned and many fine palaces were built.

Stroll through the historic city centre and explore the picturesque Piazza Erbe with the Romanseque Rotonda di San Lorenzo or the shopping avenues Via Roma and Corso Umberto I. Mantua's culinary traditions have been heavily influenced by the nearby Emilia region making it a sought-after destination for gourmets.

SIGHTSEEING

PALAZZO DUCALE

The imposing walls of the Palazzo Ducale encompass a medieval fortified tower with eight structures, several courtyards, terraces and hanging gardens. It is a veritable city within a city: through the years (from mid 15th century to the beginning of the 17th century) every successive Gonzaga duke made their own additions to the complex. Unfortunately, one of the largest art collections in Europe was later lost.

What remains – apart from the impressive rooms – is the fabulous fresco painted by Andrea Mantegna in two stages in 1465 and 1474 in the tiny, famous *Camera degli Sposi (book in advance for the Camera on tel. 04 12 41 18 97 or at www. ducalemantova.org)*, the "Wedding Room". The fresoces depict the Marquis Ludovico, with his wife and court as he waits for his son Francesco who has just been appointed cardinal; he has learnt the news in a letter that he holds in his hands. Mantegna's way of representing the interaction between his characters and his trompe l'oeil techniques were remarkable and the Camera degli Sposi soon became an example for many other European royal courts. *Tue–Sun 8.15am–7.15pm | 6.50 euros | Piazza Sordello 40 | www.ducalemantova.org*

PALAZZO DEL TÈ

Huge giants support the arches and tumbling rocks: there's plenty going on in the frescoes with which Giuliano Romano decorated some of the halls in the summer residence of the Gonzagas on the southern edge of the city in 1535. And the festivities they held were also pretty spectacular. *Mon 1pm–7.30pm, Tue–Sun 9am–7.30pm (in winter to 6.30pm | 12 euros | Viale Tè 13 | www. palazzote.it*

FOOD & DRINK

ANTICA OSTERIA AI RANARI

Like going back in time: down-to-earth landlords, rustic wooden tables and genuine Mantuan traditional fare. Try the deep-fried frogs or *risotto alla pilota*, rice cooked to the bite with sausage. closed *Mon | Via Trieste 11 | tel. 03 76 32 84 31 | www.ranari.it | Budget–Moderate*

L'OCHINA BIANCA

Excellent Mantuan cuisine, typical of the area are dishes prepared with pumpkin, rice as well as fried fish. *Closed Mon | Via Giuseppe Finzi 2 | tel. 03 76 32 37 00 | www.ochinabianca.it | Budget–Moderate*

WHERE TO STAY

CASA DEL TEATRO

Friendly accommodation in three enchanting, elegant rooms in the middle of the old town. Also an extremely generous breakfast. *Piazza Teofilo Folengo 3 | tel. 36 69 70 39 01 | www.casadelteatro. it | Budget*

HOTEL BROLETTO

A small, charming hotel at the heart of the old town. *14 rooms. | Via Accademia 1 | tel. 03 76 32 67 84 | www.hotel broletto.com | Budget–Moderate*

Thunderstorm of the gods: Jupiter hurls lightning in Mantua's Palazzo del Tè

INFORMATION

Piazza Mantegna 6 | tel. 03 76 43 24 32 | www.turismo.mantova.it

WHERE TO GO

CURTATONE (141 F5)

Some 9 km/5.6 mi to the west, on the banks of the Mincio, is the small hamlet of Curtatone with its pilgrimage church *Santa Maria delle Grazie* in the Renaissance style. The church is famous for its unique INSIDER TIP papier-mâché votive figures that look down into the church from niches. Dozens of Madonna painters also meet in front of the church in the middle of August. Make a point of going to the *Locanda delle Grazie (Mon–Thu evening, closed Tue/Wed)| Via San Pio X 2 | tel. 03 76 34 80 38 | Budget–Moderate)* so you can try one of their delicacies such as the delicious as *tortelli di zucca*.

SABBIONETA ★ (141 E5)

Ideas like this could only come true during the Renaissance: in 1554 Vespasiono Gonzaga decided to show his conceited Mantuan cousins a thing by building the ideal Renaissance city – from scratch. The result is charming Sabbioneta, about 35 km/21.8 mi south-west of Mantua, on a loop of the Po River. Here he created his own court complete with Palazzo Ducale and theatre (Teatro Olimpico), art gallery and parade ground, churches, monasteries and palaces (some of them beautifully painted) all secured by a fortified wall. The interior can only be viewed with a guide: *daily 9.30am–1pm and 2.30pm–5pm, April–Oct until 6.30pm | 12 euros | at the Ufficio Turismo | Piazza d'Armi 1 | tel. 0 37 55 20 39*

PAVIA

(140 B5) The magnet is the magnificent Carthusian monastery a few miles north of the gates of Pavia. And the town (pop. 73,000) itself? An old royal city.

Many medieval kings were here before us, the Lombards, Charles the Great, and the Holy Roman Emperor Henry II, who was crowned King of Italy here in 1004. Pavia still has something of the Middle Ages about it today, with its narrow streets and venerable churches such as the Roman basilica of *San Michele* and the church of *San Pietro in Ciel d'Oro* (1132), which contains the mortal remains of Sant'Agostino, the great religious teacher of early Christianity. The completely straight Corso Strada Nuova runs through the city centre: from the *castle* (with the city museums) near the station to the loveliest river bridge in northern Italy, the *Ponte Coperto* that crosses the Ticino, both built in the 14th century, the era of the Visconti dukes of Milan. After its destruction in WWII, the covered bridge in red-brown brick was rebuilt exactly as before. The *university* is also on the Corso (14th–18th centuries), one of the oldest in Europe. Walk across elegant courtyards to reach the maze of the lecture halls, some of which are decorated with frescoes. The rice used for risotto grows in the green, watery surrounding area. And you can enjoy a bowl of it – as well as crispy pizzas and the view of the impressive brick-built *cathedral* – at the pizzeria ☘ *Hosteria Regisole (daily | Piazza Duomo 4 | tel. 03 82 53 09 20 | Budget–Moderate)*. Information: *Via del Comune 18 | Palazzo del Broletto | tel. 03 82 07 99 43 | www.vivipavia.it*

WHERE TO GO

CERTOSA DI PAVIA ★ (140 B4)

Just under 10 km/6.2 mi north of Pavia, the splendid Certosa di Pavia rises up like a crown from the swampy marshlands. The Carthusian monastery, which looks like a castle, was built in 1390 by the Duke of Milan, Gian Visconti to accommodate the family mausoleum. A century later the magnificent marble façade of the church was added. Beautiful courtyards and monastic cells can be

The full splendour of the Renaissance: cloister in the Certosa di Pavia

viewed. Certosa is usually rather crowed during the weekends. *Tue–Sun 9am–11.30am and 2.30pm–4.30pm, May–Sept until 6pm | admission free (donation requested)*.

After all this very fine art and architecture, you can also enjoy some fine dining in the old abbey mill: in the elegant restaurant *Locanda Vecchia Pavia Al Mulino (closed Son evening and Mon | tel. 03 82 92 58 94 | www.vecchiapaviaalmulino.it | Moderate–Expensive)*.

INSIDER TIP ▶ LOMELLINA (140 A–B 4–5)

You experience a completely different sense of Italy with a trip through the rice fields of Lomellina, which are flooded at the end of April, remain under water until July and harvested during September. At the gourmet festival *Sagra del Riso*, during mid June in Sannazzaro de' Burgondi, you can sample several different risotto dishes. Some rice farmers offer direct sales such as the *Azienda Agricola Zerbi (Via Roma 69 | www.risozerbi.it)* in the village *Pieve Albignola*, where you can get the best Carnaroli, the rice used for risotto. And in *Mortara*, you can buy first-class goose salami and ham made at the *Corte dell'Oca Palestro (Via Francesco I Sforza 27 | www.cortedelloca.com)*.

OLTREPÒ PAVESE (140 B–C 5–6)

Beyond Tincino and the motorway the hilly landscape and vineyards of the Oltrepò Pavese (which means 'beyond *(oltre)* the Po') starts 20 km/12.4 mi south at Stradella. One of the centres of wine is *Santa Maria della Versa* 11 km/6.8mi south of Stradella. Just outside the town, on the SP45, is the *Trattoria Mondo Piccolo (closed Mon | Ca' Nova-Sannazzaro | tel. 0 38 57 91 69 | Moderate)*: an extremely basic "little world", but the food is supreme: first-class ham, nettle

risotto, excellent meat and home-made desserts, and the wine is from nearby vineyards.

VIGEVANO ★ (140 B4)

Shoes and a famous square: these two symbols of the town (pop, 63,500), situated on the Ticino like Pavia, simply don't go together. You can feel every little pebble that plasters the vast *Piazza Ducale* in the elegant locally-made shoes. Of course, Italy isn't exactly short of pretty squares, but this one here, a rectangle framed by Reinassance arcades, is undeniably one of the loveliest. It was built in 1494 by Duke Ludovico il Moro of the Milanese Sforza family as a festive, elegant forecourt to his castle. Two hundred years later, the cathedral was built on the opposite side of the square, effectively "rotating" its position. But that in no way detracts from its beauty – at its best at any time of day, whether over a breakfast cappuccino or an evening aperitif. You can walk through the grounds of vast *Sforza Castle* on any day of the week and up the ⚲ tower *(Tue–Sun 10.30am–12.30pm, Sat/Sun also 2pm–5pm | 1.50 euros)* for the lovely views.

Gorgeous Renaissance brocade silk shoes, high heels for Marylin Monroe or trendy Manolo Blahniks for the stars of Sex and the City are on display at the shoe museum ● *Museo Internazionale della Calzatura (Tue–Fri 2pm–5.30pm, Sat/Sun 10am–6pm | admission free | Piazza Ducale 20)* in the castle.

An excellent selection of wines, accompanied by plates of cheese and cold meats at lunchtime, with an aperitif and in the evenings is available from the modern, appealing restaurant *Vespolina (Sat- and Sun lunchtime, Mon closed | Via Cairoli 10 | tel. 03 81 68 12 85 | Moderate)*. Information: *Via Cesare Battisti 6 | tel. 03 81 69 02 69 | www.iatprolocovigevano.it*

VALTELLINA

(141 D1) **The city folk escape Milan, Brescia and Bergamo at the weekends for the valley landscape of Valtellina**.

The long valley stretches from the upper end of Lake Como and east along the Adda River, continues below the Bernina massif and up to the Stelvio Pass. People hike in the side valleys in summer and come for the skiing in winter. After a workout on the hair-raising MTB trails, recharge your batteries with a helping of delicious buckwheat pizzocheri - delicious with air-dried Bresola ham and a red, such as Sassella or Sforzato from the local vineyards. The capital of the province is *Sondrio* (pop. 21,600, 307 m/1007 ft) in the middle section of the valley. This is also where you will find the *Museo Valtellinese (Tue–Fri 9am–noon and 3pm–6pm, Sat/Sun 3pm–6pm | 6 euros | Via Maurizio Quadrio 27)* with lots of interesting information on the area's history and crafts. You can still get a feeling of the old Sondrio on a stroll through Scarpatetti. And to find out just what is on offer in the valley, visit the *Ufficio Turistico (Via Tonale 13 | tel. 03 42 21 92 46 | www.valtellina.it)*. The specialities of Valtellina include *Bitto Storico* cheese from the Val Gerola side valley, which branches south at Morbegno. Try it with a glass of good wine at the *Centro del Bitto (Via Nazionale 1 | tel. 03 42 69 00 81 | www.formaggiobitto.com)* in the pretty mountain village of *Gerola Alta*. In *Morbegno* itself the address for the cuisine of the Valtellina with a selection of good organic wines is the ⚹ *Osteria del Crotto (closed Sun evening and Mon lunchtime | Via Pedemontana 22 | tel. 03 42 61 48 00 | www.osteriadelcrotto.it | Moderate)*.

A lot of farmhouses – agriturism centres – are ideal for a holiday in nature, for instance in *Mantello* at ⚹ *La Fiorida (29 rooms | Via Lungo Adda | tel. 03 42 68 08 46 | www.lafiorida.com | Moderate–Expensive)*, modern eco-friendly architecture with a spa and good food prepared with its own products. The ancient Romans were the first to relax at the *Bagni Vecchi (www.qcterme.com/it/bormio)* thermal springs in *Bormio* (pop. 4000, 1225 m/4019 ft) in the upper Valtellina; today's guests relax in steaming pools surround by the idyllic mountains and enjoy the pampering in comfortable spa hotels. Go up higher, and things are much cheaper than elsewhere: you are in duty-free *Livigno* (1816 m/5958 ft). At these cold heights, there is snow on the ground until spring and fabulous ski runs *(www.carosello3000.com)*, ski marathons, snow parties and freeride events *(www.livigno.eu)*.

VARESE

(140 A2) **It's lovely here in Varese, with parks and charming villas from the turn of the century.**

The town (pop. 80,600) and its province earn their money with high-tech, avionics, domestic appliances and textiles. A large park contains the wonderful Baroque *Palazzo Estense* (now the town hall) and Villa Mirabello with the archaeological *Civico Museo di Villa Mirabello (Tue–Sun 9.30am–12.30pm and 2am–6pm | 4 euros)*. In the Biumo district the INSIDER **TIP** ▶ *Villa Menafoglio Litta Panza di Biumo*, is set in magnificent gardens *(Tue–Sun 10am–6pm | 13 euros | Piazza Litta 1)*. The baroque villa houses one of the largest art collections in Italy that was donated by Giuseppe Panza di Biumo to the FAI *(www.fondoambiente.it)*, Italy's largest private conservation asso-

If that's not relaxing: admiring the mountains from the steaming pools of the Bagni Vecchi

ciation, thus making it available to the general public. Exhibits include works by American minimalists, conceptual artists and contemporary artists. There is also the gourmet restaurant *Luce (daily | tel. 03 32 24 21 99 | ristoranteluce.it | Moderate–Expensive)* with a beautiful terrace. Above Varese is the INSIDER TIP *Via Sacra (www.sacromonte.it)*, a mountain path that leads to the baroque pilgrimage site *Santa Maria del Monte*. The path passes 15 chapels along the way and they are all decorated with figures and frescoes depicting the story of Jesus Christ. During the 16th and 17th century in Northern Italy *Sacri Monte* or 'sacred mountains' such as this one were created in support of the Counter Reformation, today it is a Unesco World Heritage Site. Traditional cuisine with an imaginative twist can be found in the rustic-chic *Vecchia Trattoria della Pesa (daily | Via Carlo Cattaneo 14 | tel. 03 32 28 70 70 | www.daannetta.it | Moderate)*. Information: *Piazza Monte Grappa | tel. 9 03 32 28 19 13 | www.vareselandoftourism.com*

WHERE TO GO

LAKE COMO (LAGO DI COMO)
(140 B–C 1–2)

Lake Como is a beautiful, Y-shaped, glacial lake in the Alpine foothills. It is also known as the Lario, its Latin name, and it is one of the major scenic attractions of Lombardy. The lake is fringed by delightful villages, full of beautiful villas with spectacular gardens, making it a popular and romantic holiday destination. For more information visit the tourism website *www.turismo.como.it/en*

LAKE MAGGIORE (LAGO MAGGIORE)
(140 A2)

This is the longest lake in Italy (65 km/ 40.4 mi) and it is fed by the Ticino. Unlike Lake Garda, the 'poorer' eastern shore of Lake Maggiore belongs to Lombardy, the northern section to the Swiss canton of Ticino and the western shore to the Piemont region. For more detailed information refer to the very helpful the website *www.stresa.com/borromeanislands*.

FESTIVALS & EVENTS

FESTIVALS & EVENTS

6 JANUARY

Procession from the cathedral to Sant' Eustorgio, with relics of the Three Kings.

MID JANUARY/MID FEBRUARY

See the high points of the ***Milano Moda Uomo*** and ***Milano Moda Donna*** fashion weeks with parades of the next season's fashions for men and women.

FEBRUARY

Children in particular love dressing up for ***carnival,*** which according to the Ambrosian rite goes on until the Saturday after Shrove Tuesday, when there is a procession around the cathedral square of people wearing historical costumes.

MARCH

A Sunday in the middle of the month: the ***Tredesin de Marz*** flower festival with a flower market on the Piazzale Lodi and the Porta Romana in memory of the arrival of Christianity in Milan.

On the last weekend, 50,000 and more people run the ***Stramilano marathon.***

End of March **INSIDER TIP** ▶ ***Giornate del FAI:*** churches and palaces that are not normally open to the public open for a short time.

APRIL

During the first half of April, the important art fair ***Miart*** *(www.miart.it)* displays modern and contemporary works, and there are also lots of related events all over the city.

In the middle of April, designers come from all over the world for the ***Salone Internazionale del Mobile*** furniture fair, which presents all kinds of furniture and accessories. The ***Fuorisalone,*** which takes place at the same time with designer events and shows all over the city, attracts almost more visitors.

The ***Milan–San Remo Spring classic cycling race*** takes place on the last Saturday in April

MAY

Middle of the month: ***Arte sul Naviglio*** – artists display their works along the banks of the Naviglio Grande and in the galleries.

At the ***Piano City Milano*** *(www.pianocitymilano.it)* piano festival, which takes place around the third weekend in May, there are three days of concerts in parks, courtyards, cloisters, palazzi, on industrial sites and in railway stations.

JUNE

The first Sunday is the day of the ***Festa dei Navigli,*** a festival with all kinds of stands

and stalls along the Naviglio Grande and Naviglio Pavese.

Festa dei Balon in Abbiategrasso outside the gates to Milan on the Naviglio Grande with a large bonfire and plenty of risotto and wine

JULY/AUGUST
During the holiday, the city organises various ***open-air events*** (cinema and music) in courtyards, on squares and in parks.

SEPTEMBER
MI-TO: a festival of unusual concerts at unusual venues around Milan and Turin. *www.mitosettembremusica.it*
Le Vie del Cinema: all of the films of the Venice, Locarno and Cannes film festivals The beginning of the month brings the world of Formula 1 with screaming engines and Ferraris for the ***Italian Grand Prix*** in Monza.

At the end of the month the whole city waits with bated breath for the new spring and summer fashions at the ***Milano Moda Donna***.

END OF OCTOBER–END OF NOVEMBER
New music sounds at ***Milano Musica*** *(www.milanomusica.org)* in museums, theatres and galleries, and plenty of concerts for the ***Jazzmi festival*** *(www. jazzmi.it)*.

DECEMBER
The season at La Scala opens on St. Ambrose's Day with a ***gala premiere***; crowds gather around the stalls that have been set up for the INSIDERTIP ***Oh Bej oh Bej*** festival around Sant'Ambrogio.

PUBLIC HOLIDAYS

1 Jan	*Capodanno*
6 Jan	*Epifania*
March/ April	*Pasquetta* (Easter Monday)
25 April	*Liberazione* (Liberation Day)
1 May	*Festa del Lavoro*
2 June	*Giorno della Repubblica* (Republic Day)
15 Aug	*Ferragosto*
1 Nov	*Ognissanti*
7 Dec	*Sant'Ambrogio* (day of the patron saint of Milan)
8 Dec	*Immacolata Concezione* (Immaculate Conception)
25 Dec	*Natale*
26 Dec	*Santo Stefano*

LINKS, BLOGS, APPS & MORE

www.vogue.it/en Italian Vogue's website includes detailed photo spreads and videos about the current fashion shows in Milan

www.hellomilano.it The online magazine of the English-speaking community in Milan publishes detailed information on events, exhibitions, guided tours of the city and so on. Similar: www.aboutmilan.com Everything you need to know about your destination at a glance: history, events, virtual tours, current news and offers

milano.mentelocale.it and www.milanodabere.it The websites of two city magazines (but only in Italian) with current cultural events, trends, festivals, places of interest, restaurants, pubs, bars, ice-cream shops and more

www.milancity.com A city website that offers a wealth of information about current events, museums, restaurants and cultural events

www.theblondesalad.com This blog belongs to Italy's most famous fashion blogger, Chiara Ferragni who is from Milan, and is an insider's take of the street and fashion scene in Milan.

www.fashion-crowd.blogspot.com A Milan magazine editor shares the favourite places of her friends and colleagues in the fashion industry: the blog archive is a treasure trove of listings of restaurants and shops in Milan and the surrounding areas. In English and Italian.

www.thesartorialist.com Photographer and blogger Scott Schuman has a unique eye for street style: he is forever finding fabulous characters on the streets of Milan

www.thechicfish.com Until the end of 2016, designer Anna Carbone and photographer Giovanni Gennari shared their passion for charming/morbid retro and vintage style here, and their finds, primarily in Milan, in the way of fashion, pubs, places, shops, events, pictures and so on. The archive is still a treasure trove!

Regardless of whether you are still researching your trip or are already in Milan: these addresses will provide you with more information, videos and networks to make your holiday even more enjoyable

www.italiangoodnews.com The mission of this communications agency is to report good things from Italy, such as what is happening on the Italian start-up scene

https://www.instagram.com/uccellina03/?hl=de A young Englishwoman living in Milan posts the pretty pictures she takes on her strolls around the city on Instagram

www.bikedistrict.org A visit to this community is essential for anyone exploring Milan on a (borrowed) bike. **INSIDER TIP** Brilliant: an English-language interactive route planner for bike rides through Milan that provides metre-by-metre information on the conditions of the routes etc.

VIDEOS & MUSIC

www.youtube.com/watch?v=XkInkNMpl1Q A brilliant five minute clip 'Europe and Italy' by the comic book artist and animator Bruno Bozzetto that demonstrates in a few minutes just how different the Italians are from the rest of Europe

www.youtube.com/watch?v=LewfJxhzup0 The clip is 'A Day in Milan' and it is a virtual tour of the city including the main shopping streets. The soundtrack is the famous pop song 'L'Italiano' by Toto Cutugno

https://www.youtube.com/watch?v=IIFU96eEZHE an elegiac sequence of Milan images made up of street scenes, sights and people that is a lovely introduction to the city

APPS

Milano Metro This app with lots of functions will help you to find your way around on Milan's Metro network, and shows you where your nearest station is

Spotted by Locals – Milan Locals' Tips This clever app takes you off the beaten tracks to the favourite spots of the Milanesi

citymapper.com/milano An app that instantly and easily compiles any desired subway, bus and tram route in Milan

info.openwifimilano.it Use this Internet site to log onto the city's WiFi network free of charge

TRAVEL TIPS

ARRIVAL

If you are travelling to Milan by car from the UK, an attractive route is to go via Dijon to Chamonix and then head for the Mont Blanc Tunnel and continue into the Aosta Valley and past Como to Milan. In good weather an alternative to the tunnel is the Grand St Bernard Pass. Coming from Germany and Austria the route would be via the Brenner motorway (Brenner–Verona–Modena) to Milan. There are several busy motorway ring roads *(tangenziali)* that extend around Milan with over 20 bypass roads leading to parts of the city or the *centro*. Try to avoid arriving during rush hour when the traffic on the major roads is often at a standstill.

There are direct connections to Milan from European cities via France, Switzerland (Basel–Milan), Germany or Austria (Eurocity Munich–Verona–Brenner) they arrive in the main train station Stazione Centrale, north-east of the city centre. If you are arriving from within Italy you may have to change from a suburban train to get to the central station. *www.raileurope.co.uk* and *www.fsitaliane. it/homepage_en.html* and *trenitalia.com*

International flights usually land at the large Milano Malpensa Airport 50 km/31.1 mi north-west of the city, occasionally also at Milano Linate (mainly internal Italian flights). The low-cost airline operators use the small Orio al Serio near Bergamo. Information for Linate and Malpensa: *tel. 02 74 85 22 00 | www.sea aeroportimilano.it, for Orio al Serio: tel. 0 35 32 63 23 | www.sacbo.it.*

Linate and Malpensa are connected to the Stazione Centrale by a direct bus ("Terravision" or "Malpesa Shuttle"). Linate: bus terminal at the station on the Piazza Luigi di Savoia side, approx. every 30 min between 6am and 11pm, travel time 25 min, 5 euros per route, tickets on board; or take the ATM bus no. 73 from Corso Europa (Piazza San Babila) between 5.30am and 0.20am. Malpensa: bus terminal Piazza Luigi di Savoia, two lines, every 10–20 min between 3.45am and 0.30am, travel time around 60 min, 10 euros, *www.malpen sashuttle.it, www.terravision.eu* or *www. autostradale.it;* or take the commuter train Malpensa-Express *(www.malpensaexpress. it)* from Stazione Nord (Cadorna), stopping at the main station and Stazione Porta Garibaldi every 30 min (every 20 min at peak times) between 5.50am and 11pm, travel time approx. 40 min, 13 euros. Orio al Serio: buses to and from Milan (Stazione Centrale) between 4am and 11pm, travel time up to 50 min, 4 euros, *www. orioshuttle.com, www.autostradale.it.*

RESPONSIBLE TRAVEL

It doesn't take a lot to be environmentally friendly whilst travelling. Don't just think about your carbon footprint whilst flying to and from your holiday destination but also about how you can protect nature and culture abroad. As a tourist it is especially important to respect nature, look out for local products, cycle instead of driving, save water and much more. If you would like to find out more about eco-tourism please visit: *www.ecotourism.org*

From arrival to weather

Your holiday from start to finish: the most important addresses and information for your Milan trip

BICYCLES

Milan has a good network of public rental bicycles; in the city centre there are over 100 pick up/drop off BikeMi stops where you can rent or return one of the 1500 orange-coloured bicycles. A fee of 2.50 euros is charged for a day. The first hour is free, thereafter, every hour costs 50 cents. Information and registration: *tel. 8 00 80 81 81 | www.bikemi.com* or at the ATM, the information point of Milan's transport services near the cathedral square (quite a high credit card deposit). You can also hire a bike by the hour or day at *Rossignoli (133 F4) (Ø J3) (Corso Garibaldi 71)* in the centre, or at *Bike Rental (Piazza Sempione 6 | www.2cicli.com)* on the Arco della Pace. The urban cyclist scene meets at the bike café **INSIDER TIP** Upcycle *(0) (Ø O2) (closed Sun and Mon evenings | Via André-Marie Ampère 59 | www.upcyclecafe.it)*, calculate routes with *www.bikedistrict.org*.

CAMPING

At the western outskirts of the city there is a basic camping site that also offers bungalows; there are caravan and tents sites under the trees – lots of mosquitoes in summer though. The site is near the exhibition centre and the *Gardaland* Waterpark that is open from June to early September. *Camping Village Città di Milano (0) (Ø 0) (Via Gaetano Airaghi 61 | tel. 02 48 20 70 17 | www.campingmilano. it | Metro 1 De Angeli, then bus 72)*

CAR HIRE

Many rental companies have offices at the airports or at the Stazione Centrale. A small car costs upwards of 60 euros per day while a car in the compact class will cost you upwards of 160 euros for a weekend.

BUDGETING

Espresso	about £1/$1.50	for a cup at the counter
Wine	from £2.70/$3.70	for a carafe of wine (¼ L)
Snack bar	from £3.50/$4.90	for a panino
Exhibition	from £4.50/$6.10	for admission
Metro	£1.30/$1.80	for a trip
Shoes	from £195/$270	for a handmade pair of men's shoes

CONSULATES & EMBASSIES

BRITISH CONSULATE GENERAL
Via San Paolo 7 | tel. +39 02 72 30 01 | Metro Duomo | ukinitaly.fco.gov.uk/en

U.S. CONSULATE GENERAL MILAN
Via Principe Amedeo 2/10 | tel. +39 02 29 03 51| Metro Turati | https://it.usembassy.gov/embassy-consulates/milan/

CUSTOMS

EU citizens can import and export goods for their personal use tax-free (800 cigarettes, 1kg tobacco, 90L of wine, 10L of spirits over 22% vol.). Visitors from other countries, including those travelling to Milan via Switzerland, must observe the following limits, except for items for personal use. Duty free are: max. 50g perfume, 200 cigarettes, 50 cigars, 250g tobacco, 1L of spirits (over 22% vol.), 2L of spirits (under 22% vol.), 2L of any wine.

DRIVING

On roads outside built-up areas dipped-beam lights are required during the day. If your car breaks down outside of towns it is compulsory to wear a safety vest when leaving the vehicle. Maximum speed: on the motorways 130 km/h/80 mph, expressways 110 km/h/68 mph, on highways 90 km/h/56 mph and in suburban areas 50 km/h/31 mph. The alcohol limit is 0.5. Milan's city centre is a designated "green zone" (with a congestion charge) from Monday to Saturday between the hours of 7.30am and 7.30pm (6pm on Thursday) within the Cerchia dei Bastoni ring roads ("Area C"). All emission standards for petrol vehicles from euro 1 and from euro 4 for diesel vehicles also require an *Ecopass (5 euros/day)*. It is available from e.g. tobacconists, newspaper kiosks, ATMs and ticket machines in inner-city multi-storey car parks. The receipt for the congestion charge must be on clear view in the car. Information at *www.comune. milano.it/wps/portal/ist/en/area_c*. There is a charge for parking in blue areas (3 euros/hour, max. 2 hours), parking tickets *(gratta sosta)* are available from parking wardens, at machines and in tobacconists. White zones are reserved for residents with a parking permit. Day visitors are better off parking outside Area C or on the outskirts of the city on one of the car parks near the subway stations — such as Lampugnano, Cascina Gobba, Famagosta, San Donato, Rogoredo. For more information on the congestion charge, on car parks such as locations, addresses, prices, connections to public transport, go to the website of the municipal transport services: *www.atm-mi. it*. A good app for the right subway or tram: *citymapper.com/milano*.

EMERGENCY SERVICES

Toll free emergency call for police and rescue services *tel. 112;* breakdown services *tel. 80 31 16* or *tel. 8 00 11 68 00*.

HEALTH

In the case of an emergency you can get around the clock outpatient treatment at the *Pronto Soccorso* or *Guardia Medica (tel. 800 103 or 118)* where you are treated free of charge e.g. at the *Ospedale Fatebenefratelli* (134 A3) *(ⵂ K2) (Corso*

FIT IN THE CITY

Two popular running tracks are in the north-western part of the city: the urban forest *Bosco in Città* and the large Parco di Trenno, both can be reached with bus 72 or via the arterial road, Via Novara. The cycle path or *pista ciclabile*, along Via Melchiorre Gioia, Via Emilio de Marchi and Vai Padova along the Naviglio Martesana towards Vimodrone and to Cassano d'Adda (there and back 60 km/ 37.3 mi, *www.bicimilano.it*), is a nice trip into nature. Summertime means swimming, surfing, canoeing and sailing on the artificial lake *Idroscalo* near the Linate airport. There are a dozen *Get Fit (www. getfit.it)* fitness centres all over the city.

di Porta Nuova 23). Chemists that are open at night: *Piazza del Duomo 1* and at the main station.

INFORMATION

ITALIAN STATE TOURISM BOARD (ENIT)
– *1 Princes Street | Mayfair, London | tel. 020 74 08 1254 | info.london@enit.it*
– *686 Park Avenue | New York, NY | tel. 01 212 245 5618 | newyork@enit.it*
– *365 Bay Street, Suite 503 | Toronto | tel. 01 416 925 4882 | toronto@enit.it*

INFORMATION IN MILAN
The *Urban Center* (131 D3) (*ᄊ K4–5*) *(daily 9am–7pm, Sat/Sun until 6pm | Galleria Vittorio Emanuele II/ Piazza della Scala | tel. 02 88 45 55 55 | www.turismo.milano. it)* is the tourist information in the city centre, where you can also buy the *Milano Card (7 euros (24 hours), 13 euros (48 hours), 19 euros (72 hours) | www. milanocard.it)*, which gets you discounts in some of the museums or for some concerts and free travel on public transport.

INFORMATION ON THE INTERNET
You'll find the first important information at *www.turismo.milano.it*: the portal of the Città Metropolitana Milano contains lots of information, details of current events and apps. Information is also available on the commercial websites *www.milanofree.it* and *www.ciaomilano. it*. A good summary of highlights and events is given on *www.wheremilan.com* and (Italian only) *vivimilano.corriere.it*.

INTERNET ACCESS & WIFI

You can get online free of charge at many places in the city centre – at stations, in some public buildings, on squares, in cultural facilities. Register at *info.openwifimi lano.it* or on an ATM machine. Lots of cafés offer free *WiFi*, and most hotels will give you a password free of charge at reception.

MEDIA

Milan is Italy's largest newspaper city and there are almost a dozen daily newspapers published here. For visitors the most important papers for event information

CURRENCY CONVERTER

£	€	€	£
1	1.10	1	0.90
3	3.30	3	2.70
5	5.50	5	4.50
13	14.30	13	11.70
40	44	40	36
75	82.50	75	67.50
120	132	120	108
250	275	250	225
500	550	500	450

$	€	€	$
1	0.80	1	1.25
3	2.40	3	3.75
5	4.00	5	6.25
13	10.40	13	16.25
40	32	40	50
75	60	75	93.75
120	96	120	250
250	200	250	312.50
500	400	500	625

For current exchange rates see www.xe.com

are the 'Corriere della Sera' (weekly overview and tips every Wednesday in 'Vivi Milano') and 'La Repubblica' ('Tutto Milano' every Thursday). 'Corriere della Sera' is also available online in English. Major television stations are the public government broadcaster RAI, the private Mediaset (Berlusconi) and La 7 (also private). Regionally there are also various smaller broadcasters.

MONEY & CREDIT CARDS

ATMs *(bancomat)* are available everywhere and most credit cards are accepted by hotels, filling stations and departments stores, as well as restaurants and shops.

PHONE & MOBILE PHONE

The area code in Italy is part of the telephone number and must always be dialled (including the zero!). The international dialling code for Italy is *0039*. Dial *0044* for calls from Italy to the UK; *001* to the USA. Buy a telephone card *(scheda telefonica)*, at kiosks and *tabacchi* shops. A local call during the day will cost 10 cents/min. for land lines and mobile phone numbers from 20 cents, calls abroad from 50 cents. A prepaid Italian card is more cost effective. You can buy cards from 5 euros in telephone and tobacconists. To keep your mobile phone and internet rate as low as possible speak to your service provider about rates beforehand.

POST

Stamps (75 cents for standard letters and postcards within the EU) can be bought in most tobacconists.

PUBLIC TRANSPORT

Single tickets *(biglietto ordinario)* are available from most kiosks, tobacconists and vending machines in the Metro stations. They cost 1.50 euros (for use in the city limits) and are valid for 90 minutes from validation, and trams and buses may be used in all directions, the Metro though only for one ride (changing possible). If you want to use the Metro after taking the bus or tram, you have to have your ticket validated again at the Metro entrance. A day ticket *(biglietto giornaliero)* for all the transportation options costs 5.70 euros. The card has a magnetic strip and is simply swiped at the validating machine or on the buses and trams. A 24-hour ticket *(biglietto giornaliero)* for every form of public transport costs 4.50 euros, and 8.25 euros for 48 hours. If your ticket has a magnetic strip, just draw it through the endorser at the turnstile or on buses or trams. There was talk of an increase in prices at the time of going to press. Information at *www.atm.it/en* and at ATM points *(Mon–Sat 7.45am–8.15pm)* at the larger Metro stations. Milan's transport services have very good Apps that can be downloaded from their site, which you can then use to choose the necessary transport. The fourth and fifth Metro lines are under construction but the first sections will be opening soon. Apart from the Metro there are also some city train lines which cross the sprawling city. Buses to the surrounding areas, to other Italian cities and to other countries depart from the bus terminal at the *Metro station Lampugnano* ((0) (*M B1*) | Metro 1 | schedules: www. autostradale.com). Regional trains *(www.trenord.it)* connect the towns of Lombardy.

SIGHTSEEING TOURS

Bus tours by *City Sightseeing Milano* (130 B2) (*M J4*) *(summer daily 9.30am–5.25pm approx. every 30min, winter 10am–4.15pm every 75 min from Piazza Castello | 25 euros/48 hours | www.mila no.city-sightseeing.it)* with commentary, duration 90 minutes, can also be used with the hop-on hop-off principle.

The tourism websites *www.turismo.mila no.it, www.wheremilan.com* and *www. aboutmilan.com* contain lots of offers for guided tours with multi-lingual guides on special events, exhibitions and topics. Guided tours on Segways are offered by *www.segwaytourmilan.com (Via Rovello 1a)*. The four-hour guided bike tours of the city with *www.bikeandthecity.it*, *www.bikemymilan.com* and *altervista.org are worthwhile, friendly and not too expensive.* Or cruise **INSIDER TIP** on your own on a Milanese tram for 1.50 euros: many of the inner-city lines still use the originals from the 1930s. Or take the tram no. 9, which travels the inner-city ring Cerchia dei Bastioni.

TAXI

Taxis in Milan are white. The minimum fare is 3.30 euros, kilometre rate from 1.28 euros and a supplement is charged after 10pm, on Sundays/public holidays and for extra luggage. Call a taxi at: *tel. 02 40 00* or *02 53 53.*

TIPPING

Rule of thumb: five to ten per cent, if you were satisfied with the service. In the restaurant you leave the tip on the table after you have received your change.

WHEN TO GO

Milan has a continental climate with cold, wet winters and warm summers. Milan is protected by the Alps so it seldom gets bitterly cold, however the moisture in the Po Valley often makes the winters damp and the summers oppressively sultry (mosquitoes!). Fog and mist are also common. But do not worry: Milan also has bright, clear days. The best time to travel is in the spring and late summer or early autumn. The many trade fairs and fashion or design weeks cause hotel prices to rocket on those days (for dates of the trade fairs go to *www.fieramilano.it*).

WEATHER IN MILAN

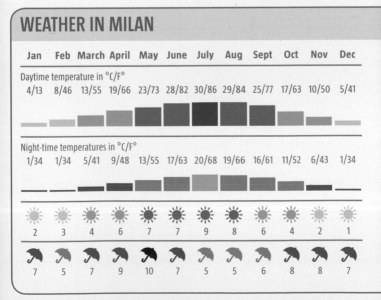

	Jan	Feb	March	April	May	June	July	Aug	Sept	Oct	Nov	Dec
Daytime temperature in °C/F°	4/13	8/46	13/55	19/66	23/73	28/82	30/86	29/84	25/77	17/63	10/50	5/41
Night-time temperatures in °C/F°	1/34	1/34	5/41	9/48	13/55	17/63	20/68	19/66	16/61	11/52	6/43	1/34
☀	2	3	4	6	7	7	9	8	6	4	2	1
☂	7	5	7	9	10	7	5	5	6	8	8	7

USEFUL PHRASES ITALIAN

PRONUNCIATION

c, cc	before e or i like ch in "church", e.g. ciabatta, otherwise like k
ch, cch	like k, e.g. pacchi, che
g, gg	before e or i like j in "just", e.g. gente, otherwise like g in "get"
gl	like "lli" in "million", e.g. figlio
gn	as in "cognac", e.g. bagno
sc	before e or i like sh, e.g. uscita
sch	like sk in "skill", e.g. Ischia
z	at the beginning of a word like dz in "adze", otherwise like ts

An accent on an Italian word shows that the stress is on the last syllable. In other cases we have shown which syllable is stressed by placing a dot below the relevant vowel.

IN BRIEF

Yes/No/Maybe	Sì/No/Forse
Please/Thank you	Per favore/Grazie
Excuse me, please!	Scusa!/Mi scusi
May I ...?/Pardon?	Posso ...? / Come dice?/Prego?
I would like to .../Have you got ...?	Vorrei .../Avete ...?
How much is ...?	Quanto costa ...?
I (don't) like that	(Non) mi piace
good/bad	buono/cattivo/bene/male
broken/doesn't work	guasto/non funziona
too much/much/little/all/nothing	troppo/molto/poco/ tutto/niente
Help!/Attention!/Caution!	aiuto!/attenzione!/prudenza!
ambulance/police/fire brigade	ambulanza/polizia/vigili del fuoco
Prohibition/forbidden/danger/dangerous	divieto/vietato/pericolo/pericoloso
May I take a photo here/of you?	Posso fotografar La?

GREETINGS, FAREWELL

Good morning!/afternoon!/ evening!/night!	lunedì/martedì Buon giorno!/Buon giorno!/
Buona sera!/Buona notte!	venerdì/sabato
Hello! / Goodbye!/See you	Ciao!/Salve! / Arrivederci!/Ciao!
My name is ...	Mi chiamo ...
What's your name?	Come si chiama?/Come ti chiami
I'm from ...	Vengo da ...

Parli italiano?

"Do you speak Italian?" This guide will help you to say
the basic words and phrases in Italian.

DATE & TIME

Monday/Tuesday/Wednesday	lunedì/martedì/mercoledì
Thursday/Friday/Saturday	giovedì/venerdì/sabato
Sunday/holiday/working day	domenica/(giorno) festivo/(giorno) feriale
today/tomorrow/yesterday	oggi/domani/ieri
hour/minute	ora/minuto
day/night/week/month/year	giorno/notte/settimana/mese/anno
What time is it?	Che ora è? Che ore sono?
It's three o'clock/It's half past three	Sono le tre/Sono le tre e mezza
a quarter to four	le quattro meno un quarto/ un quarto alle quattro

TRAVEL

open/closed	aperto/chiuso
entrance/exit	entrata/uscita
departure/arrival	partenza/arrivo
toilets/ladies/gentlemen	bagno/toilette/signore/signori
(no) drinking water	acqua (non) potabile
Where is ...?/Where are ...?	Dov'è ...?/Dove sono ...?
left/right/straight ahead/back	sinistra/destra/dritto/indietro
close/far	vicino/lontano
bus/tram	bus/tram
taxi/cab	taxi/tassì
bus stop/cab stand	fermata/posteggio taxi
parking lot/parking garage	parcheggio/parcheggio coperto
street map/map	pianta/mappa
train station/harbour	stazione/porto
airport	aeroporto
schedule/ticket	orario/biglietto
supplement	supplemento
single/return	solo andata/andata e ritorno
train/track	treno/binario
platform	banchina/binario
I would like to rent ...	Vorrei noleggiare ...
a car/a bicycle	una macchina/una bicicletta
a boat	una barca
petrol/gas station	distributore/stazione di servizio
petrol/gas / diesel	benzina/diesel/gasolio
breakdown/repair shop	guasto/officina

FOOD & DRINK

Could you please book a table for tonight for four?	Vorrei prenotare per stasera un tavolo per quattro?
on the terrace/by the window	sulla terrazza/ vicino alla finestra
The menu, please	La carta/il menù, per favore
Could I please have ...?	Potrei avere ...?
bottle/carafe/glass	bottiglia/caraffa/bicchiere
knife/fork/spoon/salt/pepper	coltello/forchetta/cucchiaio/sale/pepe
sugar/vinegar/oil/milk/cream/lemon	zucchero/aceto/olio/latte/panna/limone
cold/too salty/not cooked	freddo/troppo salato/non cotto
with/without ice/sparkling	con/senza ghiaccio/gas
vegetarian/allergy	vegetariano/vegetariana/allergia
May I have the bill, please?	Vorrei pagare/Il conto, per favore
bill/tip	conto/mancia

SHOPPING

Where can I find...?	Dove posso trovare ...?
I'd like .../I'm looking for ...	Vorrei .../Cerco ...
Do you put photos onto CD?	Vorrei masterizzare delle foto su CD?
pharmacy/shopping centre/kiosk	farmacia/centro commerciale/edicola
department store/supermarket	grandemagazzino/supermercato
baker/market/grocery	forno/ mercato/negozio alimentare
photographic items/newspaper shop/	articoli per foto/giornalaio
100 grammes/1 kilo	un etto/un chilo
expensive/cheap/price/more/less	caro/economico/prezzo/di più/di meno
organically grown	di agricoltura biologica

ACCOMMODATION

I have booked a room	Ho prenotato una camera
Do you have any ... left?	Avete ancora ...
single room/double room	una (camera) singola/doppia
breakfast/half board/full board (American plan)	prima colazione/mezza pensione/ pensione completa
at the front/seafront/lakefront	con vista/con vista sul mare/lago
shower/sit-down bath/balcony/terrace	doccia/bagno/balcone/terrazza
key/room card	chiave/scheda magnetica
luggage/suitcase/bag	bagaglio/valigia/borsa

BANKS, MONEY & CREDIT CARDS

bank/ATM/pin code	banca/bancomat/ codice segreto
cash/credit card	in contanti/carta di credito
bill/coin/change	banconota/moneta/il resto

HEALTH

doctor/dentist/paediatrician	medico/dentista/pediatra
hospital/emergency clinic	ospedale/pronto soccorso/guardia medica
fever/pain/inflamed/injured	febbre/dolori/infiammato/ferito
diarrhoea/nausea/sunburn	diarrea/nausea/scottatura solare
plaster/bandage/ointment/cream	cerotto/fasciatura/pomata/crema
pain reliever/tablet/suppository	antidolorifico/compressa/supposta

POST, TELECOMMUNICATIONS & MEDIA

stamp/letter/postcard	francobollo/lettera/cartolina
I need a landline phone card/ I'm looking for a prepaid card for my mobile	Mi serve una scheda telefonica per la rete fissa/Cerco una scheda prepagata per il mio cellulare
Where can I find internet access?	Dove trovo un accesso internet?
dial/connection/engaged	comporre/linea/occupato
socket/adapter/charger	presa/riduttore/caricabatterie
computer/battery/rechargeable battery	computer/batteria/accumulatore
internet address (URL)/e-mail address	indirizzo internet/indirizzo email
internet connection/wi-fi	collegamento internet/wi-fi
e-mail/file/print	email/file/stampare

LEISURE, SPORTS & BEACH

beach/bathing beach	spiaggia/bagno/stabilimento balneare
sunshade/lounger/cable car/chair lift	ombrellone/sdraio/funivia/seggiovia
(rescue) hut/avalanche	rifugio/valanga

NUMBERS

0	zero	15	quindici
1	uno	16	sedici
2	due	17	diciassette
3	tre	18	diciotto
4	quattro	19	diciannove
5	cinque	20	venti
6	sei	21	ventuno
7	sette	50	cinquanta
8	otto	100	cento
9	nove	200	duecento
10	dieci	1000	mille
11	undici	2000	duemila
12	dodici	10000	diecimila
13	tredici	½	un mezzo
14	quattordici	¼	un quarto

STREET ATLAS

The green line indicates the Discovery Tour "Milan at a glance"
The blue line indicates the other Discovery Tours

All tours are also marked on the pull-out map

Photo: Piazza Cordusio

Exploring Milan

The map on the back cover shows how
the area has been sub-divided

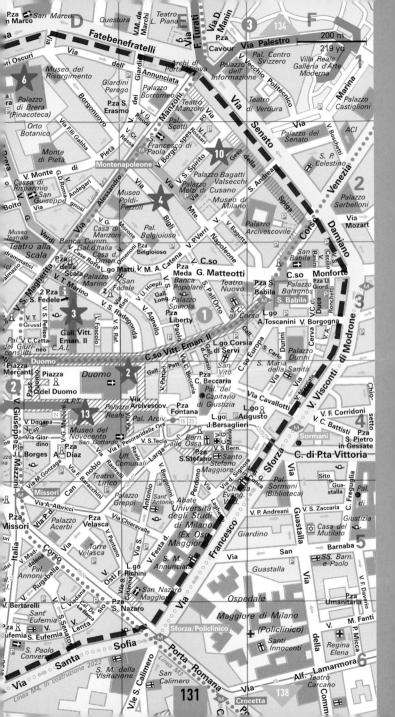

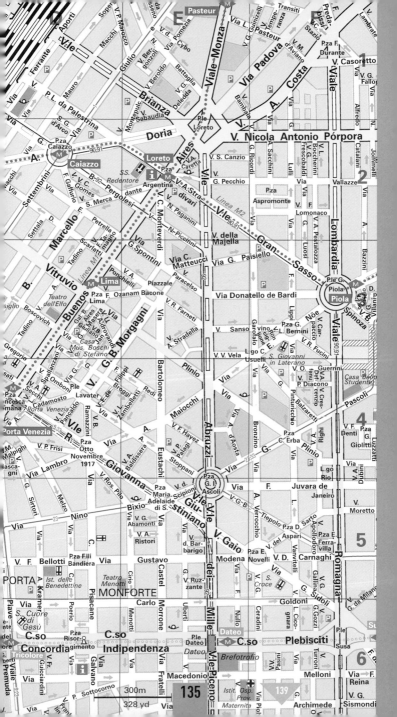

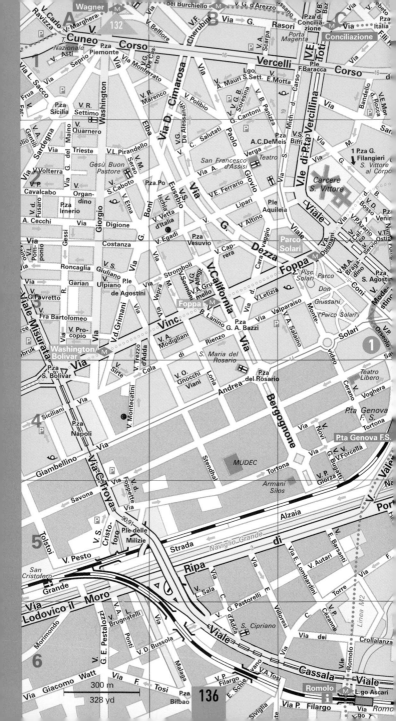

STREET INDEX

KEY TO STREET ATLAS

Autostrada / Autobahn		Motorway / Autoroute
Strada a quattro corsie / Vierspurige Straße		Road with four lanes / Route à quatre voies
Strada di attraversamento / Durchgangsstraße		Thoroughfare / Route de transit
Strada principale / Hauptstraße		Main road / Route principale
Altre strade / Sonstige Straßen		Other roads / Autres routes
Informazioni / Information	**i**	Information / Information
Parcheggio / Parkplatz	**P**	Parking place / Parking
Ostello della gioventù / Jugendherberge	▲	Youth hostel / Auberge de jeunesse
Via a senso unico / Einbahnstraße		One-way street / Rue à sens unique
Zona pedonale / Fußgängerzone		Pedestrian zone / Zone piétonne
Ferrovia principale con stazione / Hauptbahn mit Bahnhof		Main railway with station / Chemin de fer principal avec gare
Altra ferrovia / Sonstige Bahn		Other railway / Autre ligne
Metropolitana / U-Bahn	M ••••	Underground / Métro
Tram / Straßenbahn		Tramway / Tramway
Chiesa - Chiesa interessante / Kirche - Sehenswerte Kirche		Church - Church of interest / Église - Église remarquable
Sinagoga / Synagoge	✡	Synagogue / Synagogue
Ufficio postale - Posto di polizia / Postamt - Polizeistation	●	Post office - Police station / Bureau de poste - Poste de police
Monumento - Torre / Denkmal - Turm	♂	Monument - Tower / Monument - Tour
Ospedale - Autobus per l'aeroporto / Krankenhaus - Flughafenbus	⊕ **B**	Hospital - Airport bus / Hôpital - Bus d'aéroport
Caseggiato, edificio pubblico / Bebaute Fläche, öffentliches Gebäude		Built-up area, public building / Zone bâtie, bâtiment public
Zona industriale - Parco, bosco / Industriegelände - Park, Wald		Industrial area - Park, forest / Zone industrielle - Parc, bois
Cimitero - Cimitero ebraico / Friedhof - Jüdischer Friedhof	+ + + / L L L	Cemetery - Jewish cemetery / Cimetière - Cimetière juif
Confine della città / Stadtgrenze		Municipal boundary / Limite municipale
Zona con limitazioni di traffico / Zone mit Verkehrsbeschränkungen	⊏ ⊏ ⊐	Restricted traffic zone / Circulation réglementée par des péages
Giro avventura 1 / MARCO POLO Erlebnistour 1		MARCO POLO Discovery Tour 1 / MARCO POLO Tour d'aventure 1
Giro avventura / MARCO POLO Erlebnistouren		MARCO POLO Discovery Tours / MARCO POLO Tours d'aventure
MARCO POLO Highlight	★1	MARCO POLO Highlight

MARCO POLO TRAVEL GUIDES

Travel with
Insider
Tips

INDEX

This index lists all sights and museums in Milan as well as places and destinations in Lombardy featured in this guide. Numbers in bold indicate a main entry.

WRITE TO US

e-mail: info@marcopologuides.co.uk
Did you have a great holiday?
Is there something on your mind?
Whatever it is, let us know!
Whether you want to praise, alert us
to errors or give us a personal tip –
MARCO POLO would be pleased to
hear from you.
We do everything we can to provide the
very latest information for your trip.

Nevertheless, despite all of our authors'
thorough research, errors can creep in.
MARCO POLO does not accept any
liability for this. Please contact us by
e-mail or post.
MARCO POLO Travel Publishing Ltd
Pinewood, Chineham Business Park
Crockford Lane, Chineham
Basingstoke, Hampshire RG24 8AL
United Kingdom

PICTURE CREDITS
Cover photograph: Galleria Vittorio Emanuele (gettyimages/ Cultura Travel: W. Zerla)
Photos: awlimages: M. Bottigelli (flap right, 100, 104, 113), F. Iacobelli (98/ 99); awlimages/ ClickAlps: M. Bottigelli (30); DuMont Bildarchiv: Krewitt (114), Mosler (17); R. Freyer (25, 45, 46, 116 top); gettyimages/Cultura Travel: W. Zerla (1 top); R. M. Gill (10, 34, 96, 97); Hotel Bulgari (83); huber-images: G. Cozzi (128/ 129), G. Croppi (4 top, 26/ 27), D. Erbetta (5, 7), Gräfenhain (12/ 13, 37), S. Raccanello (93); Laif: Blickle (72), F. Blickle (81); Laif/ contrasto: Pavesi (76/ 77); mauritius images/ age fotostock: W. Zerla (flap left); mauritius images/ AGF/ M. Chapeaux (84/ 85), D. La Monaca (94); mauritius images/ Alamy (2, 4 bottom, 11, 14/ 15, 23, 40, 42, 58 right, 59, 70/ 71, 90), D. Fracchia (115), P. Gislimberti (69), Godong (6), Marka (8, 56), E. Marongiu (19 top, 62), G. Masci (20/ 21), R. Sala (33); mauritius images/ Alamy/ ASK Images: E. Marongiu (65); mauritius images/ Alamy/ Isaac74 (60/ 61); mauritius images/ Alamy/ Pacific Press/ Live news: G. Piazzolla (19 bottom); mauritius images/ Alamy/ SFM Stock 3 (114/115); mauritius images/ Axiom Photographic: M. Silvan (9); mauritius images/ CuboImages (18 bottom, 78), M. Bella (50/ 51, 55), Bluered (103), E. Buttarelli (18 top, 18 centre, 49); mauritius images/ Cultura (3); mauritius images/Travel Collection/ : C. Körte (52); T. Stankiewicz (116 bottom); H. Wagner (58 left); E. Wrba (96/ 97, 106, 109, 116, 117)

2nd edition 2019 – fully revised and updated
Worldwide Distribution: Marco Polo Travel Publishing Ltd, Pinewood, Chineham Business Park,
Crockford Lane, Basingstoke, Hampshire RG24 8AL, United Kingdom. Email: sales@marcopolouk.com
© MAIRDUMONT GmbH & Co. KG, Ostfildern
Chief editor: Marion Zorn; author: Henning Klüver, co-author: Bettina Dürr; editor: Christina Sothmann
Programme supervision: Lucas Forst-Gill, Susanne Heimburger, Johanna Jiranek, Nikolai Michaelis, Kristin Wittemann, Tim Wohlbold
Picture editors: Gabriele Forst; What's hot: Bettina Dürr, wunder media, Munich
Cartography street atlas & pull-out map: © MAIRDUMONT, Ostfildern
Cover design, p. 1, pull-out map cover: Karl Anders – Büro für Visual Stories, Hamburg; design inside:
milchhof:atelier, Berlin; p. 2/3, Discovery Tours: Susan Chaaban Dipl.-Des. (FH)
Translated from German by Wendy Barrow and Mo Croasdale
Editorial office: SAW Communications, Redaktionsbüro Dr. Sabine A. Werner, Mainz: Julia Gilcher, Cosima Talhouni, Dr. Sabine A. Werner; prepress: SAW Communications, Mainz, in cooperation with alles mit Medien, Mainz
Phrase book in cooperation with Ernst Klett Sprachen GmbH, Stuttgart, Editorial
by PONS Wörterbücher

MIX
Paper from
responsible sources
FSC® C124385

DOS & DON'TS 👆

Tips to help you avoid everyday pitfalls in Milan

DON'T COUNT YOUR MONEY ON A BUS

In crowded places anywhere – such as markets or at a railway station – you must expect to encounter pickpockets. Busy trams, buses and subways are other places where you should take care. So please don't count your change on a bus, and be sure to keep your purse or wallet in a very secure place.

DO WAIT TO BE SEATED

When entering a restaurant, or even a pizzeria, it is common to wait for a waiter who will then lead you to your table or let you choose one.

DO AVOID SHOPPING IN THE CITY CENTRE ON SATURDAYS

It seems as if the whole of Lombardy comes to Milan on Saturdays. People push and shove on the pavement and those who are strolling become a hindrance. Browsing in peace is impossible and there are queues for cashiers and the ladies bathroom at the opera. Even the trams get stuck in traffic!

DON'T BE TAKEN IN BY TICKET TOUTS

Sometimes it is easier to get tickets to La Scala than for a football match between Milan and Inter. But beware, do not buy tickets from black market ticket touts *(bagherini)* that are waiting in front of the stadium. They are at the very least overpriced or worse, quite possibly fake.

DO DRESS APPROPRIATELY

In Italy it is expected that appropriate clothing (no shorts, no skimpy tops) be worn in churches and places of worship. It is also best not to walk around talking and taking photographs while religious services are in progress. You will not be allowed into the cathedral with bare shoulders or in a very short skirt.

DO TAKE THE RIGHT TAXI

When you arrive at the airport or train station you will see queues of passengers patiently waiting for taxis. Some taxi drivers scout the arrivals for their prey: newly arrived tourists. They will take you straight to their vehicle only to charge you astronomical prices once you arrive at your destination. So it's best to wait your turn at the taxi departure point like everyone else.

DON'T FALL FOR FORGERIES

Never buy anything from street hawkers at rock-bottom prices which they claim are 'genuine' Lacoste shirts, Louis Vuitton purses, Gucci bags, Rolex watches or other perfect imitations of brand articles. They are never the real thing, and since 2004 it is not only illegal to sell such items; purchasing them is also a serious crime! Spot checks are carried out, even at the airports.